Dos and Don'ts of Behaviour Management

Other behaviour management titles available from Continuum

Getting the Buggers to Behave (3rd edition)
Sue Cowley
Managing Very Challenging Behaviour
Louisa Leaman
Behaviour Management Tony Swainston
Taking the Stress Out of Bad Behaviour 3–11
Simon Brownhill
100+ Ideas for Managing Behaviour J. Young

Dos and Don'ts of Behaviour Management

2nd edition

Roger Dunn

continuum

This book is dedicated to my loving wife Valerie

Continuum International Publishing Group
The Tower Building, 11 York Road, London SE1 7NX
80 Maiden Lane, Suite 704, New York, NY 10038

www.continuumbooks.com

First edition published 2005

British Library Cataloguing-in-Publication Data
A catalogue record for this book is available from the British Library.

ISBN: 978 08264 9390 3 (paperback)

Library of Congress Cataloguing-in-Publication Data
A catalog record for this book is available from the Library of Congress.

Typeset by Aarontype Limited, Easton, Bristol
Printed and bound in Great Britain by MPG Books Ltd, Bodmin

Contents

Contents

Introduction

At the time of writing, I am into my thirty-seventh year as a teacher. Incredibly, that time has simply flown by. I can say with my hand on my heart that there is no nobler profession or a profession more important than teaching. I could argue that perhaps successive governments have not given the level of importance it deserves to it, nor to the people who are its front-line troops. However, if you do not share my belief, then it probably isn't the profession for you.

At my present school, I am Director of Behaviour. Like all schools, and certainly every school in which I have taught, there are 'challenging pupils' (get used to that phrase!) and they represent a constant challenge to all the staff who teach them, or have to deal with them around the school.

I recently completed an MSc in Educational Leadership, which was an extremely valuable and illuminating experience. For one, I had to do a tremendous amount of background reading, and two, I entered into a journey of self-reflection. One thing that occurred to me was that there is a plethora of behaviour management books on the market, many of them with excellent advice and good methodology, but not one of them really hits the mark with me. They tend to be far too wordy and concern themselves too much with mundane theory. What you really need is something direct and to the point. If I was going into teaching now, I would want a handy, easily accessible book of dos, don'ts and possible strategies that I could employ. I would want it to be easy to understand and follow and just as easy to put into practice. I would want alternatives and advice, and I would want to know that I could trust these, because they had been tried and tested in the most difficult of educational circumstances and were still being employed. I would also want a complete checklist of everything I would need to do before I stepped into the classroom, before I came into contact with my first pupil. I would also want a guide to all the other aspects of teaching that I had not even given any attention to. In short: a comprehensive, easy to read, straight to the point book I could dip in and out of as and when.

If you are considering teaching as your chosen profession, this book will give you concise advice on everything you will need to know and do in a wide range of circumstances: from problems with individual pupils, to a classroom 'riot', to how to mark, as well as ensuring you are perfectly prepared at all times and know how to bring this about successfully. All of these have either a direct or indirect impact on the behaviour management of pupils, as I shall outline as I proceed.

As you read this book, you will see overlaps and points that resonate throughout. This is quite deliberate: very little practical advice that I shall give you stands in glorious isolation. It will also serve to underline key pointers and hopefully, in this way, begin to inculcate the very common-sense and well-tried methods that do work. And please remember, and forgive me for being prosaic so soon, I am coaching you and new techniques need to be practised in the teaching sense just as much as in any sporting sense you can conjure up. Do not give up if it doesn't work straightaway: persevere and grow in confidence and trust me: it will score for you too!

I repeat that this is a wonderful, rewarding and incredibly important profession. You owe it to your own sanity and to the education of those in your charge to be as good as you can at it.

This book can be used by anyone going into or already in teaching, whether they are primary or secondary based. It is as germane to a teacher in this country as it is to any teacher in any country in the world. Teaching is a universal art; it does not significantly change from one country or culture to another, but the principles remain the same. I am a secondary school teacher, but that does not mean that my experiences preclude those in the primary sector. My wife is a primary school teacher and has read this through for me; you have the benefit of her many years of primary experience also. However, where I mention different classes or teaching groups, I appreciate that this is not germane to the primary sector. The advice is though, as are all the guiding principles; so all you primary sector teachers don't be put off.

I wish you well and sincerely hope that what you are about to read will be an ongoing useful tool that you will refer to time and again to enable you to become the teacher who you really want to be and who all the pupils, whom you will teach, deserve and need you to be.

1 Making the Decision

There were four things I seriously considered taking up as a career. One was sport. I had the opportunity of playing professional cricket, but there just wasn't the money in the game and I never felt that I was good enough to make it all the way to the top and play internationally. I was considered for semi-professional football, but I got married, moved away from that area and didn't try again. One career in sport down! A career treading the boards was also a possibility. I did main drama at teacher training college and there were plenty of opportunities to take up a career as an actor when I finished. Ditto as for cricket: not enough money in it unless you get to the very top. Two down! I have the actor in my blood and love the cut and thrust of argument and debate; so a career as a barrister appealed. Problem: too footloose and fancy free at 19 to consider working that hard and having to study so intensely. Three down! The fourth was teaching. And actually it combined all four of them in one package:

Dos and Don'ts of Behaviour Management

I have taught sport, run teams (football, basketball, cricket), I have taught drama and written, directed and produced scores of plays in schools (and if you want to be a success in front of pupils, you need to have the good actor somewhere in your blood), and I also get to hold court in both classroom and staffroom.

However, the most important thing that you need is confidence. This is the one absolute attribute that you have to take into the classroom. Without it, you are already on the back foot. Pupils smell fear, indifference and nervousness. They begin to assess and weigh you up the first second they clap eyes on you. They make their calculations based upon these initial observations. How you stand, how you walk, the way you carry yourself. Be under no illusion, look weak and timid and already some of them will have started licking their lips. Be unsure and uncertain and you are already at a disadvantage. It is not about size or colour or shape, it is about the way you come across, and that must be as confident, composed, and most importantly, in control.

If you are reading this because you are considering a career as a teacher, you need to ask yourself: 'Do I think I have these attributes?' You need to do a self-assessment, because if you do not possess them naturally, you are going to have to acquire them. One of the tasks we did many years ago at Drama College was looking at how people walked and what it said about them. It made me analyse how I walk myself. Head up, shoulders back and a measured pace with not too big a step, comes across as being in control, confident and reassuring. Conversely, small hurried steps, head down, shoulders hunched, give off the exact opposite vibes. Of course there are combinations of the examples mentioned and each one gives off a different message about that person. I tried my hardest to walk like the first example. Obviously you can never totally change, but it is amazing how such small, seemingly insignificant things add up and make such a significant difference. Try it for yourself: observe those around about you and apply some of the principles I have mentioned above to try and assess how they come across to you as a result, and see if you agree with what I am saying. The aim here is to give you what sports people call 'the edge'.

How good a talker are you? I can talk for my country ('More is the pity!' I can hear friends and colleagues chorus). But believe me, the ability to talk is a major advantage in teaching. This does not preclude people who are naturally quiet. But they cannot be 'quiet' in a classroom and the ability to talk, and talk well, is a fundamental necessity, because much of your teaching depends on it as a means of communication. And it is not just being able to talk: can you talk clearly so that pupils can understand what you are saying? Do you have a strong regional accent that would be difficult for those outside of that region to understand? Can you modify it? Is it going to be a problem for you if you teach outside of your region, or indeed for pupils in that region who are not locals?

Dos and Don'ts of Behaviour Management

Do you like children? This seems an almost absurd question, but you might be amazed by how many teachers I have met in my time who really dislike youngsters. It's a bit like having arachnophobia and working with spiders for a living! A fundamental liking for and interest in youngsters is so important. They will try you, frustrate you, wear you to a frazzle at times, but if you understand, sympathize and even empathize, you will have the patience, tolerance and forbearance to 'touch base' with them and ultimately succeed. And they will know this, believe me; never underestimate how important you are going to be, or already are, in many of their lives, and taking a real and genuine interest in them as people will reap huge dividends.

Are you well organized? Trust me; this is no profession for those who are not. Being confronted by a class of pupils is not the time to discover that you've left your overheads at home, or that you haven't brought any spare paper or pens, or you really don't know what you're going to teach in that lesson. Yes, it does happen! And it mustn't happen to you, especially in the first weeks and months. Train yourself now! Tidy up your room at home and put things in order. Get used to filing things neatly away in clearly labelled folders. If you don't have a diary, buy one and start recording key dates in it and get used to using it at least twice daily: at the start and the end of each day. This must become a habit. You will learn about other good habits later on in this book, but this is one that will have a positive effect even outside of the school and is one that you can train yourself to do now.

Are you a good planner and organizer? It is not just teaching that requires these two attributes, most professions do. However, in teaching you will have to constantly plan and organize. Good teachers tend to be excellent at both, in and out of the teaching environment. Again, you can train yourself. You need to be able to think ahead, commit ideas and thoughts to writing, revise, change as required and then act logically on what you have devised. The committing to writing is all important. Get used to doing that now with anything and everything you are planning and organizing: holidays, parties, night out, etc. Get used to making lists and filing them away (see above) for future reference. Don't always rely on the PC; you do need the paper hard copy as well for easy reference or for when the PC is not operational, a not uncommon occurrence in the school situation! Whilst on the topic of technology: do not rely on it solely in teaching, because it will let you down and it always seems to do that when you are most under pressure and confronted by your most challenging pupils. You will need a back-up: make sure you have that back-up to hand.

2 The Psychology of Teaching

A classroom can sometimes feel like a battle-zone, with you as the teacher entrenched on one side of the room and the pupils dug in on the other. Like major battles, they generally start with a few skirmishes. In military terms, skirmishers are the soldiers who go in front of the main army and test out the opposition's defences. You will meet these in the classroom: they are the pupils who will be testing your defences from the second they meet you.

And of course, just as in the military situation, these skirmishers are going to shy well away if they are confronted by a well-armed, battalion-strength force, which is prepared, bristling with fire power, confidently standing its ground, clearly anticipating every eventuality and obviously up for the battle. Pupil skirmishers are no different: they will observe what is in front of them and make their decisions accordingly.

As I mentioned in the previous section, pupils sense nervousness and they feed on your uncertainty, and a point to really take on board is that when you start teaching, they are the ones on familiar territory: it is their ground not yours. The senior pupils in that school will have been there for five years in a primary and four in a secondary school! Only pupils who start the school when you do will be on equal terms with you. For the rest of the pupils, they will know the layout of the school, be familiar with all the nooks and crannies and be up to all the little ruses.

So be prepared for all of this. Do not go like a lamb to the slaughter into the lion's den. Remember: you are the adult! You are in charge! You know what you are doing! And they are going to see that the instant they clap eyes on you. Stand tall, look them in the eyes, be business-like, be professional and start as you mean to go on. And if you do, you will have already won round one of the battle. And round one is the most important, because it is very difficult to win the other rounds if you lose that one. That very first registration, that very first lesson with a new group is all important: essential even.

And finally: keep a sense of proportion, and this is of huge significance and relevance, because aspiring teachers can get the impression (haven't I just given it?) that the majority of the pupils will be against them. This is simply not true, even in the most undisciplined of schools with a plethora of challenging pupils. The miscreants in all schools are very much in the minority. However, they too frequently cause problems disproportionate to their number and if you do not keep the

Dos and Don'ts of Behaviour Management

situation in focus, you can pretty soon feel beleaguered and battle weary. So remember: most of the pupils do want to learn and do want to impress you – they do, really! Get that majority on your side and bring them along with you and you will be psychologically in a good frame of mind, because you know that you are doing a worthwhile job for most of the pupils in your care. So with the majority of youngsters on your side and you literally thanking and praising them at every opportunity for being so, we move on with a little more confidence and a little less trepidation.

3 The Pro-active Essentials of Managing Pupils

The Six Ps

Forget 'Who Dares Wins' as the SAS motto; if you've read any of the many books written by ex-members of this elite special forces group, you will know that it should read 'Perfect Planning and Preparation Prevents Poor Performance'. (The SAS have another 'P' before 'Poor'; you can guess what it is!) In teaching, I have my own spin on the six Ps: 'Failing to Plan = Planning to Fail!' What this means is that before you even attempt any of the many strategies I am going to outline for you in this book, you will already be at a serious disadvantage in terms of controlling the behaviour of your pupils if you do not read, digest and carry out the following advice closely. Only highly experienced and excellent teachers can get away with ad lib lessons, and then it is largely because of both their experience and the relationship that they have developed with the pupils in their charge, which may well have come about over a considerable period of time.

Again it has always amazed me that many of the teachers I have known over the years who have had the most problems engaging with youngsters have been those whose planning and preparation have been the poorest. So being prepared, well planned and organized has as much to do with behaviour management as anything else you are going to read, because it is the foundation upon which all else will hopefully be built.

I shall give some examples of poor preparation and planning. The teacher arrives at her/his class and then realizes that s/he has not photocopied enough sheets for the pupils and so has to leave the classroom to get more done. The teacher has a difficult group of disaffected pupils. These pupils rarely bring equipment to class and teacher has forgotten to bring spare pens. The lesson requires a television and a video recorder/ DVD player, but the teacher does not know what the video channel number is or it needs a remote control device and this is missing. There are 28 pupils in the class and the teacher has brought a half set of text books assuming that there will be enough for one textbook per two pupils. However, there are only 13. The teacher has mislaid her/his whiteboard marker and cannot write up essential parts of the lesson. And a classic: the teacher has everything perfectly set up to show the class a video or DVD on some aspect of biology. The class are settled and seated in an orderly semi-circle around the television. The teacher presses the play button on the video or DVD and 'Match of the Day' music blares out followed by Gary Lineker and Alan Hansen welcoming the pupils to the programme! The correct video was still at home. Yes, it really happened! And so did the chaos that ensued.

The list is virtually endless and is repeated every lesson in every school every day by some teacher or other. Some teachers can get away with it, many cannot! Make sure you are not one of them! I know that it seems a lot to think about to begin with, but eventually it will become second nature. And content yourself with the simple thought that if you have these things in order, your chances from the outset of being successful will be exponentially enhanced.

Putting the Six Ps into practice

1. Check you have all the equipment you need for every lesson that day: pens, pencils, rulers, erasers, paper, a sufficient number of textbooks, exercise books, folders, whiteboard marker and rubber, chalk and blackboard duster, etc
2. Check that you have any other equipment you need: overhead projector, overheads, TV, video/DVD player, the cassette, CD player, the CD(s), etc.
3. Check that all of this equipment you will be using works.
4. Check where the electrical sockets are in the room and if they all work.

Dos and Don'ts of Behaviour Management

5. Think about the arrangement of the class if they are watching some kind of video presentation: taller pupils at the back, smaller at front, etc.
6. Have any electrical equipment you are going to be using in the lesson already set up and ready to use.
7. Make sure you know how to operate any electrical equipment (interactive whiteboards, DVDs, video recorders and knowing which is the video channel are infamous examples!).
8. Check that you have a key to the classroom or that it will be open (especially important if you do not have your own classroom – very common in the secondary sector).
9. Wherever possible, be at the door of the classroom before the pupils arrive to greet them and ensure an orderly entrance into the room.
10. If they are there before you, make sure you establish a routine with them: it might be that they must wait in the corridor and have coats already removed; you might allow them to go into the room, but they must have their coats removed and books and equipment already out on their desks.
11. Make sure you have a class list and mark book.
12. Make sure you have organized a seating plan.
13. Make sure you have an up-to-date Special Needs register for your classes.
14. Make sure you have an up-to-date Gifted and Talented register for your classes.
15. Make sure you have prepared a differentiated lesson.

16. Make sure you have extension work for the more able pupils.
17. Make sure you have support work for the less able.
18. Make sure you have a 'Late Sheet'.
19. Make sure you know what the school's systems are for dealing with pupil misbehaviour.

You are probably reeling a little now, but this is all about being organized and having some self-discipline. Any one of the above not being fulfilled can potentially lead to a disaster at worst, disruption at best. You train yourself properly and the good habits will become second nature. Make a copy of the above list and then photocopy additional copies. Have one on you at all times and use it! You could even put one in your diary. Many of the above could form a key part of your lesson planning. I have numbered them here, rather than have them as bullets points, so for quite a number of them you can simply put the relevant number on your lesson plan to remind you that that is what you need to check up on. This saves time and effort. Time is a major factor in teaching and anything you can do to save it is vital.

Many of the above are self-evident and just plain common sense. Getting used to them is simply inculcating good habits into your everyday routines. However, the more challenging the pupils, the more each one becomes even more significant and can make the difference between you getting to the end of the class intact or you being taken apart.

Dos and Don'ts of Behaviour Management

Here are some important 'Dos and Don'ts', and reasons why, that stem from the Six Ps list:

* *Do get the small things right.* All pupils are facing you; pens, pencils and other objects that they can play and fidget with are put away; make them sit up straight; make them look at you. Say: 'Right class, sit up straight and look this way, please!' This focuses their attention on you; it is business-like and sets an immediate upbeat tone for the rest of the lesson. And you will be amazed at how it works! It immediately puts you in control and sends that message, signalling to them that you are someone who is in control. If they have pens on the table and you do not need them to use them immediately say: 'Put pens, pencils and any other objects away immediately please!' When they comply, say: 'Thank you!' Do it precisely, very business-like and confident and you have already got the pupils to obey a couple of very simple, straightforward instructions, and in this way have instantly and simply set a positive tone for the rest of the lesson.

* *Do carry a supply of pens for those pupils who do not have any.* It never ceases to amaze me that teachers do not do this, and there is then an immediate confrontation with the very pupils with whom you least want to have a confrontation. You may need to buy these pens yourself in extreme circumstances, but whatever it will cost you will be worth every

penny! Buy pens with removable tops. When you lend them out, take the top off and put it on your desk: pen tops on desk = number of pens lent out. For pencils and rulers and the like, you can either make a note of how many you have lent out or you can have a monitor to be responsible for doing the handing out and collecting in for you. Pupils are very adept at doing this. Some teachers go in for a more elaborate method, because they are sick and tired of always being a pen or pencil down each lesson. This method is to have the class list and/or seating plan in front of them and then put a code letter next to each pupil who has borrowed anything: *Pn = pen; Pl = pencil; R = ruler; E = eraser* and so on. And oh yes, before I forget, most pupils utter these immortal words when they want to borrow something: 'Can I lend a pencil, please?' To which most teachers reply: 'Yes, you can, but I appear to have enough, thank you!' Resist this temptation, unless you have a really good relationship with the class. However, do correct their misuse of English – remember: you are a teacher after all! One other point to remember here is to constantly spell out expectations to your pupils. You expect them to have equipment with them, even if you are not going to turn it into an issue and a confrontation when they do not.

- *Do have spare A4 lined and unlined paper with you for the pupil who has not brought in or has 'lost' her/his exercise book.* Again, avoid the potential confrontation with pupils at the very moment you want to get on with the lesson. It is the same type of pupil who is likely to have 'forgotten' her/his book, and the one who is going to test you by being late to the lesson or by looking for any opportunity to misbehave.

- *Don't make a big issue over late-comers.* There are three categories of late-comer: first category, genuine reason for being late, not a problem pupil; second category, constant late-comer and this is one of many ways in which s/he will bring about a confrontation with you; third category, same as second category, only these pupils will sometimes arrive extremely late to your lesson, possibly even showing up when you have done all the opening preparation and introduction.

  Follow these steps for late-comers:
  - Get all late-comers to put their name on the Late Sheet.
  - *Do NOT stop the lesson to deal with them!* At the end of the lesson as everyone is packing away, have a word with them then. Make sure the whole class can both see and hear this. You are wanting to make sure it is known that lateness is something you will not tolerate in future and that defined sanctions will occur next time.
  - *For persistent late-comers you will need to have a punishment:* break time detention, letter home, referred to a head of year, etc.

- For the late-comer who has missed the introduction to your lesson, you need a copy of that to give to her/him. This needs to be simple to understand. When you are ready, you can go over and give a brief verbal explanation also.
- Keep a couple of desks empty near the door into the classroom for late-comers; this will stop them walking across the room attracting an 'audience'.
- Remember expectations: 'I expect you to arrive on time in future to my lessons.'

♦ *Do not have your back turned to the class for more than a few seconds.* Too many teachers write out lengthy work on black or whiteboards. There is too much room for misbehaviour when your back is turned – avoid it! Either write this out before the lesson, or have it prepared on sheets for distribution.

♦ *Do take a register every lesson (not necessary in primary school) where you read out each of their names and expect a 'Yes, Miss', 'Yes, Sir' or (what I prefer) a 'Yes, and your surname'; in my case 'Yes, Mr. Dunn'.* This begins the lesson in a formal, organized and settled manner.

♦ *Do learn the names of each pupil in each of your classes as quickly as possible.* Knowing a pupil's name makes the job of checking their behaviour that much easier and more effective.

♦ *Do have a seating plan.* This will help you to use and learn their names. Remember, this also helps with the distribution of pens, pencils, etc. as I have already mentioned.

♦ *Do make eye contact with every pupil in your class every 45 seconds.* Pupils get used to this and are much less likely to stray away when you are talking to them as a class. The pupil who is not looking at you should expect you to ask her/him a question. They'll soon get used to this. A good adage to put to youngsters is: 'You listen with your eyes! You hear with your ears.' I don't know how many hundreds of my pupils will have that embedded forever in their consciences! The important thing is – it works!

♦ *Do take time to learn the school systems for dealing with poor behaviour.* Every school is different and it is vital that you familiarize yourself with all of these systems before your first encounter with any youngster. Not knowing these systems, and even worse not being able to apply them, puts you in a vulnerable and disadvantageous position.

♦ *One of the school systems will almost certainly be detention.* You cannot detain pupils for any length of time whatsoever at lunch time or at the end of the day, unless you have informed a parent/carer of your intention to do so. This is of real importance and many schools forget this and have a nominal 'ten minutes' at the end of sessions. These are not legal! I remember having to deal with a group of angry parents whose Year 7 daughters/sons had missed the bus home on a wet winter's evening. Consequently they walked, and on the way home they were chased by a gang of youths. The teacher had only kept them behind for seven or eight minutes, but it was enough to make them miss their bus. If anything had happened to any of those youngsters, that teacher would have been responsible. Break time detention is ideal, because you do not have to let a parent/carer know about it. The best way to handle this in a secondary school is to ask the teacher who is teaching the lesson before break to either bring the pupil to you or to remind the pupil of the detention.

Nothing Succeeds like Success

You have probably heard the old joke: what succeeds? Answer: a toothless budgie! And you probably didn't laugh then either. Quirkily, it always brings a smile to my face and the beauty of being a teacher is that there is always a new cohort of youngsters to tell it to! But being successful is important to all of us in all our walks of life; one thing that I have endeavoured to do in this book is to underline the simple fact that youngsters are just younger versions of us with the same feelings, hopes and wishes. Our job as educators is to nurture, to encourage, to help, to support and to assist in the process of producing gainful, positive citizens from our young charges. And youngsters, like us, will not reach any of this if they do not taste success and taste it regularly and are then made fully aware of it.

Consider this: think of the times as an adult you have been presented with something completely new. It could be new technology; it could be a new way of doing something; it might be new initiatives in teaching! The list is endless. Have you ever struggled? Have you ever felt like giving up or worse, actually given up? Take computers as a classic example. I can remember Archimedes computers coming into schools in the 80s. I had an Amstrad word processor and that had taken me an age to get to grips with, and then only because I had a close friend who also had one and who was a computer geek, but these new Archimedes computers with their completely different writing and desktop publishing packages were a quantum leap into the unknown. I went on a course for six weeks, one afternoon a week, to learn how to use the basic packages. It took me years to master it and only because I had the support and backing of the head of ICT at school. Without him, I would have floundered and struggled and maybe given up the ghost. And just when I had finally arrived at a position of control and mastery, Mr. Bill Gates introduces PCs and Microsoft into the world! Oh joy! Back down the anaconda with only a stepladder in front of me for comfort.

Let us look more closely at the process which surrounds failure. What makes us fail as opposed to succeed? Well, not understanding something from the outset is almost certain to result in abject failure. Not having the wherewithal to actually do the task at hand, and then not being given the appropriate support structures to help you in your hour of need, will also doom you to failure, because you will almost certainly give up. Not realizing that you are actually doing quite well and that you are heading in the right direction will certainly not be of any help, because you have no point of personal reference and may just throw in the towel out of pure ignorance of your true standing.

Now we need to turn our spotlight onto the pupils in front of us and be well aware of just how they might feel if any of the above ever comes to pass for them. And trust me: it does and frighteningly all too often. Far too many youngsters are confronted with failure on a daily basis, some of them in nearly every lesson they are in. Why? Poor literacy skills will come top of the list. As a teacher you need to be au fait with what these literacy levels are in the youngsters you teach. Remember, you need to know who your special needs pupils are, as well as your gifted and talented. This should be something you take very seriously, because if you do not, there will be far too many pupils in front of you who simply cannot understand what you are trying to communicate; as a consequence they will not be able to access your lesson. In simple terms: they will fail! And it is no good simply praising them here, there and everywhere in the hope that it will compensate: youngsters are not fools; they know when they are doing well and they know when they aren't. So don't try and con them.

Dos and Don'ts of Behaviour Management

And I need to emphasize here exactly what the likely outcome of all of this will be for many of those pupils in your classes: disaffection and disruption to your lessons.

The need for praise is very important, vital even, in encouraging youngsters and exhorting them to higher and better things. See the section on 'The Use of Praise' later in this chapter. But that praise must be built around the youngsters succeeding and then building upon that success. That means carefully structuring your lessons to ensure that communication is clear and concise; that you present information in different ways, creating interest and a desire to take part; and that you employ the oldest form of teaching known to us: inculcation.

If, like me, you were taught the times table, this was almost certainly done by chanting it out as a whole class time after time after time. This is inculcation: repetition of the same information. And it works! I can do any of the tables up to 12 without a second thought; it has been drummed into me. However, we can now be far more inventive in the way that we do this, but it is important that youngsters are exposed to this kind of repetition, especially if they are amongst that group of pupils whom we know are going to struggle. If they struggle with reading, make it visual or audible. Make your opening expositions interesting and challenging and even exciting. Arouse their curiosity and stir their imaginations. This is your chance to be imaginative yourself in the way that you expose the youngsters to the learning objective for that particular lesson.

The Pro-active Essentials of Managing Pupils

Make sure that every pupil can actually achieve, no matter how little; then make sure that you know that they have achieved and that they know they have as well. That is when the praise is absolutely essential. You are celebrating their achievement, celebrating their success. I recently taught the bottom group in Year 8. This particular group created havoc in many areas of the school. They were a bonded group and, because they were not fools, they knew why they were in that group. As I have told you, when I teach groups like these (and these are the groups I am given to teach!) you have to challenge them, excite them and motivate them. And you have to make absolutely sure that they are successful.

I had a constant stream of teachers who were wheeled into the room to watch me teach these youngsters and who, I hope, picked up some strategies along the way. I always had a chat with the teachers afterwards and had a discussion with them about the lesson and what their perceptions were. The last teacher to see me teach this group was newly qualified. Her observations were very perceptive as well as personally satisfying, because she picked up that the youngsters were not patronized, that they were being taught high order English: subject, verb, predicates and that everyone of them had understood the concept and had shown this in their subsequent work. She noticed how much praise they received for being successful and was amazed at how long they remained on task, working individually in silence and how pleased they were when they had succeeded.

Dos and Don'ts of Behaviour Management

One of the teaching assistants, who helped out with a couple of the boys in another group I taught, came in one day. She could not believe the way that the youngsters responded, how much they succeeded, their willingness to stay on task and their desire to impress. The reason for her astonishment was the fact that she often sat in with this group in other lessons where there was chaos. The difference: in one lesson they are tasting real success and being praised for it; in the others they are confronted with failure. It frustrates me that there are staff in the school who believe that the pupils simply behave because they are being taught by the dreaded Mr. Dunn. Believe me, it cuts no ice with pupils over a prolonged period of time what elevated position the teacher holds in the school: if your lessons are boring and they are failing, the pupils will eventually give you the same hell as everyone else.

So, in summary: youngsters, just like us, need to be given the tools to use to be successful; they need to have success in every lesson they attend; they need to be told that they have been successful and they need to be praised for that success. It is a tall order, I know, because I've been doing it for 36 years now and resting on one's educational laurels is no good whatsoever. You have to be prepared to be self-critical, self-analytical and to seek and listen to advice and have an open mind about new initiatives that may suddenly appear on the teaching horizon.

The Seating Plan

One of the most important things to organize is a seating plan, especially when you are new into a school or you have serious concerns about some of the groupings of pupils in a particular class. There are several aspects to this and each one is essential. The first is to make sure you have class lists for each of your classes (you will only need the one if you are in the primary sector). Make sure you also have a Special Needs (SEN) register, a Gifted and Talented (GAT) register and an idea of the potential troublemakers from colleagues who have taught these pupils before.

The idea is to separate the potential troublemakers from each other (remember the two back spots at either side of the classroom are the best places for two of these troublemakers at least!). Another positive action to take is to seat the pupils in a girl/boy, girl/boy formation with a bright girl next to a less academically minded boy. Academic girls can have a very positive effect on boys, as well as helping them to learn.

Remember, this is your class and getting the pupils to sit where you want them is the first sign that you are in control. This sends a very strong message to them all and puts you in the driving seat. Do not compromise; stick to your seating plan rigidly. As time progresses, you might decide to change the seating arrangements and move key personnel, or even do a wholesale swap around. You might even want to experiment with

Dos and Don'ts of Behaviour Management

different arrangements with the furniture – but if you do, do it before the pupils arrive! There is no hard and fast rule for how a room is laid out. I have always liked the three-sided conference set-up with a space in the centre of the room, where everyone can see everyone else. The teacher sits at the head of this arrangement. However, some classrooms are just not big enough or the correct shape to accommodate this lay-out.

One thing to bear in mind when laying out your classroom is to try and avoid situations where pupils have their backs to you, which is often the case when you have four pupils around a couple of joined up tables. If you like this lay-out, make sure that pupils actually turn round in their chairs when you are talking to them. Do not talk to the backs of pupils. This is of immense importance, especially when you are delivering your opening exposition. If you cannot see a pupil's face, there is a potential problem there. I shall repeat this often: people listen with their eyes, they only hear with their ears. You cannot possibly tell if a pupil is listening to you and concentrating on what you are saying if you cannot see her/his face.

Now it is one thing having a seating plan – and another getting the pupils into it! This needs careful planning also because, if you don't, you are going to end up with a massive disturbance before you even start your lesson! You must meet and greet the class at your door and line them up quietly in the corridor. You call the names of the pupils out one at a time, and you fill the back rows in first, so that you do not have pupils blocking your view of others behind them straightaway. In this way, you have also (if you have sensibly already identified them that is) removed your potentially disruptive pupils off the corridor and into the classroom, because they will be occupying the two far corner positions. (Remember? Good!)

You need this exercise to be done quickly and efficiently and you need to insist upon silence as it is carried out. If you are really on the ball and want to send hugely important signals to this group of young-sters on your first encounter with them, you will tell them that there is an activity on each of their desks/ tables and they need to make a start on that quietly as soon as they get to their seats. And, of course, you will have that starter activity there for them (see next chapter). Make it one that does not involve the use of a pen or pencil, because it will avoid the disruptive pupil interrupting your controlled entry of the children by asking for a pen. I hope you see how it can be that such seemingly small and trivial matters can cause problems disproportionate to their apparent immediate signifi-cance. The inexperienced teacher can make scores of these small errors; even experienced teachers do too! And each one of these errors adds up! Remember the old adage: 'Look after the pennies and, the pounds will look after themselves.' It is a golden adage for all teachers.

The Lesson

Be assured of one thing: pupils do not mess around if they are interested and engaged in the lesson. If you know you have a problem group of pupils, it is essential that you attempt to make the lesson as interesting and pacey as possible. Consider this carefully and rationally and think of your own experiences. Even as mature university/college students (I shall resist any temptation here for sly comments!) you must have endured some incredibly tedious lectures. How did you feel? And there again, you will have hopefully experienced some really engaging and stimulating lectures. How did you feel then? Do you think youngsters are any different? What I am trying to inculcate in you is that a great part of behaviour management is down to what you can prepare before you even encounter the young-sters you are going to teach.

Write out a lesson plan for each lesson with your learning objectives written down and how long each part of the lesson will last and then stick to it. Youngsters are wonderfully adept at 'distracting' you and taking you away from what you want them to do, which is often work! For every lesson you teach, you need a list of key words. Ideally, these words should be displayed around your classroom, so pupils can see them and use them when and as necessary. At the start of your lesson and for each subsequent section do not spend too much time on laborious explanations: move the lesson forward briskly and break your lesson up into manageable chunks. This is especially important for boys, who in general possess a shorter concentration and attention span than girls. In short, they get bored quickly: and what is that likely to lead to?

At the beginning of the lesson, consider having a four or five minute starter activity for pupils to do as they enter the classroom. This should be relatively easy with everyone being able to do it. This engages the pupils straightaway and settles them down.

Pupils learn in different ways and you need to be aware of this. Some pupils are good at listening and writing; others like using their hands; some prefer to be physical and like to move around. An interesting fact is that standing up actually increases brain activity; so it is worth bearing in mind that legitimately involving pupils in standing at certain stages of your lesson is actually beneficial!

After the starter activity, the pupils should be able to see the learning objectives for that lesson somewhere in the room. These are what you expect them to learn in that lesson and you should constantly refer to them. In this way, the pupils can see what it is they are expected to achieve and it allows them something tangible to aim for. It gives the lesson a purpose and a direction, which is vital. At the end of the lesson, you should recap what they should have learnt, and at the start of the next lesson (after the starter activity) go quickly over what they learnt in the last session. It is uplifting to actually see pupils when they leave your room talking about what they have learnt, and even

Dos and Don'ts of Behaviour Management

the most resistant youngsters enjoy the knowledge that they have actually acquired skills or learnt something new. Everyone enjoys success, and many of the pupils who will be likely to give you grief in the classroom situation are those who rarely experience success; indeed, they are far too often in a fail situation.

The purpose of all this is to create a focus and an awareness. To illustrate this I shall recount an incident I had with a boy (a Year 10 pupil, 15 years old) who was sent to me from his lesson for refusing to do his work. He was not one of my 'usual' customers and I was quite surprised to see him. And I told him so. The interesting thing was though, that he genuinely had no idea what the lesson was actually about, what the connection with the other lessons in that subject was or what he was supposed to do. He knew what the subject was, but could not get a handle on the substance of the lesson. I gently raised this point with his teacher, and went through the content of the lesson he had prepared (there was no lesson plan!) and how it had been structured. It soon became obvious that there wasn't a focus; the lesson was haphazard and there were no learning objectives whatsoever. The boy had simply given up. When I asked to see the work that the others in the class had done, it was obvious that many in the group had simply floundered on. This pupil had put down tools; others in a less compliant group would have created a major behaviour problem.

You need to take a time out here and, before we proceed, read through the lesson plan structure again and fully understand what is going on. The methodology behind this kind of lesson structure is extremely sound and anyone observing your lessons will very much want to see it in evidence. Let's recap in bullet point form:

- What are the learning objectives for the lesson?
- These need to be on display for each lesson.
- They are what you tell the pupils they are going to learn by the end of the lesson.
- Make sure that each section of your lesson teaches to the learning objectives.
- The plenary at the end recaps what the pupils should have learnt during that lesson.

Now what about homework? You are doing yourself no favours if you do not set it. There should be a school homework policy, and there should be prescribed evenings when your subject sets homework for a particular year group. If the school does not have one, have a chat with your head of department and ask for advice. The homework ideally should extend the knowledge, the expertise and the skill of the pupils by allowing them a further opportunity to revisit what they have just learnt. If pupils have planners or diaries, make sure they write the homework down. Better still; have it written out for them to copy down. And finally, do not wait until the end of the lesson to set the homework. I always give mine out near the beginning: then it isn't

Dos and Don'ts of Behaviour Management

a rushed and apparently last-second thing (which makes it appear unimportant).

Here's a handy lesson checklist:

- Be prepared: lesson plan, all the equipment you need, photocopied sheets, etc.
- Have spare pens: if a pupil doesn't have one, lend her/ him one, do not make this into an issue during the lesson and have a quiet word at the end of the lesson.
- Be there at the start of the lesson, before pupils arrive if possible.
- Start each lesson with clear learning objectives for that session: have these written out for pupils to see so that you can refer to them.
- Think about starting the lesson with a quick starter activity to engage the pupils as they are coming into the room.
- Try not to make your opening more than six or seven minutes maximum.
- Think about setting homework early in the lesson and maybe even have it written out for them to copy into their planners/diaries/exercise books.
- Try and split each lesson into bite-size chunks, probably about ten minutes each.
- Keep the lesson 'busy': 'You've got five minutes to complete this task!' If they are well into it, that five

minutes can become very elastic! Do not interrupt and stop them if they are all on task.

♦ Have quick extension exercises ready for pupils who finish a task early.

♦ Have explanation sheets to help those who struggle, with model questions and answers on them.

♦ Wherever possible, try and insist upon a ten-minute period in each lesson where the pupils work quietly and independently. Explain why you are doing this. Again, if they are working well, be prepared to extend this time.

♦ Remember: lessons with pace and interest are less likely to be interrupted by pupil misbehaviour.

♦ At the end of each lesson, recap by going over the learning objectives again.

Be Prepared to Drive your Lesson

Pupils are no different to anyone else: if there is the chance to do as little as possible and get away with it, they will take it. Poor discipline and poor behaviour are often the result of a lesson that is poorly structured with no clear focus, and equally poorly organized and paced (recall the incident I have just related about the Year 10 pupil). The pupils end up setting their own time limits and their own work rate: both are recipes for potential trouble.

Dos and Don'ts of Behaviour Management

It was the end of the school day and I was just walking along the corridor when I espied one of our newly qualified teachers sitting alone and looking forlorn in her classroom. She was reluctant to talk, said everything was fine, but this was clearly not the case. I sat and chatted around things for a while and I suggested that the cause of her despondency was the last lesson she had taught and one which I had briefly observed, when I popped into the classroom to see a pupil. She nodded. She asked me my opinion of the few minutes I had witnessed. So I started to give my advice, which was as good for her as I hope it will be for you.

The lesson had been a practical one, with the pupils cutting and pasting various planets of the solar system into their exercise books and then annotating them. What I had observed was a lot of activity, quite a high noise level and some silliness which I very quietly re-marked on to a group of girls. So why did they achieve as little as they did, the teacher wanted to know. When she actually looked at what they had achieved and produced, it was not a great deal for an hour's lesson.

The problem was that she had allowed the pupils to set the pace; she remained passive in the backseat, when she should have been driving the lesson from the front. Here is how. First: be prepared! Split the lesson into chunks: each 'chunk' is a separate activity. Time how long it takes you to do that activity and add a little bit more for the pupils to do it. More experienced teachers will be able to judge how long to allocate for each activity much more easily. Then when you set them off on each task, you tell them how long they have got to do that task.

So: 'Right class, each of you has a sheet in front of you with nine planets in our solar system. When I tell you, I need you to cut out Neptune, Venus and Pluto and paste them onto a new page in your exercise book. This is how I want it to look.' You show them a page with the planets stuck on (this is modelling – see next chapter). Then you put that model sheet in a prominent place, so all the class can see it. You may need more than one sheet. You may need one per table. Whatever you decide, make sure you've done it beforehand!

Then: 'OK; you have got exactly seven minutes to complete that task!'

Of course, because you are well prepared and you have all the equipment ready, the pupils can get on with the task without anything missing. What you do is keep giving them a time update. 'You've had three minutes and you should have finished one of the planets by now. You have one minute left – you need to get a move on! Come on, Sally, you can't afford to waste time, you've only got a couple of minutes left!'

Clap your hands, keep them on their toes and make it a little like a competition. All of this is highly motivating for pupils. It is not dissimilar to a coach on the touchline exhorting her/his team to greater effort and achievement. The pupils will certainly see that and the tempo will pick up accordingly. Remember, if anyone finishes early, you must have something for them to do. You might get them to colour the planets in, for example. Have the colour pens ready beforehand if that is what you intend, mind you!

You then move on to the next task, the next 'chunk' of the lesson. By doing it this way, you are driving the lesson. You will find that the pupils' noise level will be very much reduced and that they will remain on task, and they will complete a whole lot more in a lot less time. Additionally, they will obtain a real sense of achievement at what they have actually completed at the end of the lesson. And, of course, you will point this out to them, congratulate them on the way that they have worked and comment on the amount that they have done. Do not forget to do that! If you want an example of this, hiking is an excellent one. I have taken scores of pupils on scores of hikes and when they are getting a little fatigued, I tell them to stop and look back at how much ground they've covered: it never fails to give them a boost. This is what you can do all the time in lessons – get them to look back at the work they have done in that lesson; it's an excellent motivator!

What in effect you are doing is setting the pace and keeping them on task and focused. If you do not do this, you will find that pupils start to wander off task and lose concentration, the noise level goes up, silliness creeps in and the end product is that they will underachieve. Not only that, the behaviour will also deteriorate and can quickly spiral out of control.

This driving of a lesson is something that you can do at any time, but it is vitally important in this type of practical lesson, where pupils appear to be on task and busy, but are actually just coasting along. My newly qualified teacher had something to think about for her next similar lesson, and it only needed those objective comments and advice as to what to do next time to get her back on track. The really gratifying thing is that I know that she will. She is already a very good teacher and, because she is prepared to ask for help and advice, and take it on board, she will get even better. Don't ever be afraid to do the same.

It is always a real thrill to help someone out, especially when they are so keen to listen, learn and put into practice as this lady was (and still is). What is even more wonderful is when they come back and tell you that it worked! It makes the job so worthwhile.

Coaching

It seems incredible to me now, but over 36 years ago I was at college and doing Drama and P.E., and was introduced to the concept of constructing a P.E. lesson which, believe it or not, is exactly the same way as many educationalists are advocating now as the way to put together and teach any lesson.

The notion of sport and coaching are synonymous: after all, people who teach sport are called coaches.

Dos and Don'ts of Behaviour Management

However, there is so much that we as teachers of any subject can learn from these people.

So there I was all those years ago, with half a dozen of my student colleagues, being shown a football lesson by the then Head of P.E. at a local Newcastle comprehensive. The boys came out and did a preliminary warm-up session for about three to four minutes (starter exercise in classroom). The teacher then had them gather round and told them what his learning objectives for the lesson were, which were how to pass and control a ball with the instep. He then demonstrated how to do this in front of the boys. This took no longer than a couple of minutes. 'Don't have them standing around watching you,' he said. 'Get them involved quickly!' He did this using one of the boys as a partner and then split the lads up into pairs and set them off to emulate the way that he had demonstrated. This is modelling, which is the essence of all good coaching.

He walked around the pairs, correcting and praising as he went, and eventually he told the lads to stop and selected a pair of boys, who were demonstrating a good level of skill at this activity, to show what they could do, thus once again underlining what he had coached. This is again modelling. This time it is peer modelling, which is very important, because it shows the rest of the class that they can actually achieve this standard too. He then proceeded to bring the boys back in and he added another technique, followed by the same routine. The second technique involved passing to a moving player using the same technique. In this way, he was incrementally increasing the skill levels and opportunity for learning at each stage of the lesson. He then did exactly the same as before: walking round, correcting as he went, eventually selecting a second pair to do some peer modelling to show what he was coaching before he gathered them back in again. Then he added in a third person as a defender, incrementally increasing the level of difficulty once more. The other thing to emphasize here is that each new skill depended on the last one to be successful. This is another aspect of incremental layering to bear in mind for your lessons.

Some of the boys were quick to pick this up and he would individually move them on to another level, whilst others still had to master the basic skills involved in the first of the tasks. You can see that he had already considered the problem of differentiation. He did not want the more able lads wasting their time doing what they could do easily, nor did he want the less able boys to be equally wasting their time attempting to reach levels they could not attain yet. He ended up with four games where the lads were only allowed two touches each. There were no goals. The lesson ended with him recapping what the lesson objectives had been and what the boys had learnt. He implored them to go down to St James' Park and watch his beloved Newcastle employ the same techniques. So there was the homework element. That was the only down part of the lesson! (Well I am a Middlesbrough supporter!)

Dos and Don'ts of Behaviour Management

You can see from what I have outlined that this was a teacher way ahead of his time. But there he was, teaching us how to teach. In fact he was coaching us by modelling what we should do. I have never forgotten that one lesson. Above all else, it has had the most profound effect upon me, and this was before I even taught my first lesson. The sad thing is that I did not employ those same wonderful techniques in the classroom for far too many years. I only did so on the sports field or in the gym! If only I had known!

Now look back at the section on 'The Lesson'. See how closely this teacher's technique meshes with what I have written. They are remarkable in their similarity. What I am also saying here is that coaching is about modelling what you want pupils to do. This is as sound a philosophy in the academic sense as it was then and is now in the physical one. All of us learn by watching and observing and then trying to copy. When it does not automatically work out for us, we need someone there to give us a helping hand: some further advice and words of encouragement and away we go again. Isn't this what good teaching is all about? And don't forget the importance of peer modelling. It gives a pat on the back to those who have mastered whatever it is, and it also allows the others to see how it is done, whilst giving them hope that they too can achieve it.

Finally and probably most importantly, the effect that this method of teaching has on the behaviour of the pupils is also of particular significance. By modelling what you want pupils to do you are setting them up to succeed, because pupils can actually see what it is they have to do. Pupils, like you and me, like to succeed; it inspires confidence in themselves and in you as their teacher. And what is even more encouraging here is that it is more likely to be your real troublemakers who will be most appreciative, as a large number of these pupils misbehave because they far too often are confronted by their own inadequacies and equally far too frequently find themselves failing.

Marking

How can marking affect behaviour management of pupils? The two hardly seem congruous, but trust me they are. Pupils need to be motivated. They need to know that you are interested in them. They need to know that you work hard for them. And you should let them know this. I frequently let my pupils know that it takes me longer to mark a set of their books than it does for any single one of them to actually do the work that I set. This makes them respect the fact that you are putting effort in for them. Of course conversely, if you are an indifferent or infrequent marker, what message is that sending out to your pupils?

Two of the sides to being a teacher that the public doesn't see are the preparation and the marking. Both are vitally important and must not be neglected. However, marking is crucial in terms of motivation and maintaining a really positive, upbeat attitude

Dos and Don'ts of Behaviour Management

amongst the pupils in the classes you are teaching. I have always stuck to what a teacher told me when I first started teaching English: no pupil should do another piece of work before the last piece has been marked. And that for an English teacher means a heavy workload and real commitment. The reason behind this philosophy is straightforward: if you want pupils to learn from their mistakes, they need to have their mistakes corrected before they do their next piece of work. If that does not happen, they will automatically make the same mistakes again. Marking to this schedule is time-consuming and arduous, but it can be done, and here are some of the ways in which it can be achieved.

Think bite-size

Don't wait until pupils have done pages and pages of work. Try not to end up taking class-loads of books home with you and turgidly going through them. Try and drip-feed your marking. In English, I would have pupils (especially boys) coming up to my desk at the end of every paragraph they had written, and I would quickly go over the key points there and then with them. I'm talking 45 seconds to a minute per pupil, and it is during the actual lesson. It is positive affirmation for them, keeps them on task, and gives them instant feedback, which is what they really want. And always a verbal: 'Well done; keep going!' It also means that the lion's share of the marking is taking place in the classroom. You have all the essential ingredients: instant, positive and verbal praise. It also means that you have established a routine in your room, which additionally gives you the opportunity to bring out that pupil who is not working or who is distracting others.

This is formative marking and has been shown to have the greatest effect on pupils because of its immediacy, which has a positive motivational effect upon them. If you are relying on summative marking (taking all the books home and simply giving the one comment and maybe mark at the end), the effect is diluted, as well as taking you a great deal more time to do.

Self-marking

This is the most obvious way of relieving the marking burden: pupils mark their own work. This has to be used sparingly, but is ideal for when you need pupils to see for themselves if they are on the right lines. It is also a good reaffirmation of what you are trying to teach them, and allows them to see where they are going wrong without any undue personal embarrassment. Tell them that this is why you are doing it. The other thing to do is to tell them only to put a tick if it's correct, but alter it if it is wrong.

Dos and Don'ts of Behaviour Management

Over the shoulder

You wander round the class and mark pupils' work as they are doing it. Again, this allows for immediacy of response from you and breaks the work up. It is formative in nature and a quiet 'Well done!' in the ear will have a motivational effect. It will also help them to stay on task. If you adopt this method, be sure to keep a weather eye on what is going on around about you. Become too immersed in one pupil's piece of work and it can easily lead to misbehaviour elsewhere. So keep looking up, glancing round and verbally checking where necessary any unwanted activity. This is sound practice and pupils will notice it too.

The final mark

They have handed in their final piece of work. Be careful not to be negative with your comments. Try and make a comment about their effort and find positives in their work. Look for repeated errors rather than all the errors. Avoid putting a mark on the work unless it is an examination piece or it is the school's policy. Marks are detrimental to every pupil other than those who are the very best. Imagine if you are constantly receiving 2 out of 10 for every piece of work! Not very inspiring, is it? If you award a mark, it will be what the pupil immediately looks for and it will probably mean that the comments you have made will not be read. What a waste of time that is! Make sure that each pupil goes over the marked work when you hand it back. This is why formative marking is more positive, because they look at what has just been marked, use it, learn from it and then move on.

Positive comments that you could use at the end of a piece of written work

- I appreciate the effort you have made in this piece of work.
- A well thought out and structured piece of work.
- Thank you for the effort you have put into this work.
- A promising piece of work.
- Effort and care shown in your work. Well done!
- Once again another excellent piece of work.
- You are showing real signs of progress.
- Your best piece of work for me yet. Well done!
- You are improving with every piece of work you do.
- I liked this enormously. Thank you!
- An enjoyable piece of writing. Well done!
- Factually excellent. Well done!
- Excellently annotated and explained.

Dos and Don'ts of Behaviour Management

Any of the above positive comments can be followed by:

+ Be sure you check your use of full stops.

+ Be careful with your handwriting though.

+ Watch out though for careless errors in your use of a calculator.

+ Be sure though to annotate your diagrams.

+ Make sure that in future you put the correct historical dates in.

+ Now go back and check your paragraphing.

+ Make sure you label each apparatus in your write-up.

And so on. If you do this, you will be having a major impact upon each and every one of your pupils. You will generate a desire to do work, because it is being rewarded by your comments. Not to do this is to demoralize and deflate pupils and create the exact opposite effect to the one desired. And on the subject of demoralizing pupils, nothing is more demoralizing than a piece of work which has been obliterated by green ink. Do NOT correct every error the pupil has made. All s/he will see is the green ink and feel that s/he is useless, irrespective of what comment you may have made. It will appear like they have a mountain to climb. This is especially germane to lower-ability pupils, who may have made an extreme effort to complete the task, only to have it marked to death! What you need to do is to pick out the repeated errors and correct them. In this way, you are drawing attention to two or three key points that the pupil can rectify. It allows the pupil to focus in on those points and put them in order. This is a manageable thing for them to do; trying to put a score of errors in order is not!

Do I mark their English as well?

First point to make here is that your school should have a marking policy and you need to check what it is. This marking policy may well direct staff to set subject homework on certain nights for certain years. This should avoid pupils being set five pieces of homework on Tuesday and none for the rest of the week! It may well direct you to mark in green ink and NOT in red. This became very popular over a decade ago, when psychologists suggested that the colour red was too threatening! The other part of the homework policy may allude to the marking of English errors in subject areas other than English.

My advice, if you are not an English teacher, is to correct all spellings of key words specific to your subject. So in Geography, if a pupil writes 'exstrary', you would correct it with 'estuary'. You may wish to draw attention to paragraphing, depending on the level of the pupil. You would not do this for a pupil of very low ability, but would certainly do it for a more able pupil who has not bothered to paragraph at all.

This throws up a very interesting fact about the transference of pupil knowledge from one subject to another. As an English teacher, I often used to get jibes from other subject teachers about how poor some of the pupils I taught were at English in their subject areas. So I did a study on this and found something quite remarkable: very able and capable pupils of mine, who used paragraphs, punctuated correctly and structured sentences with care and some skill, frequently did not do so at anywhere near the same level in other subject areas. When I questioned them about this, their replies were frank and surprising: 'Because it isn't English; it's ...' (and here they would name the subject).

So, what you need to do constantly as another subject teacher is to remind them of the importance of English in your subject area, and of the need for accuracy. This is reinforced by the way that you mark some of that English as well. As a general rule then, mark the English errors that prevent the piece of work from being successful within the context of your subject.

What you also need to be aware of are the codes employed to denote the various errors. What is vitally important here is that all pupils should have a copy of these and know what they mean. Here is a typical list of codes and their meanings. If by some incredible chance your school does not have such a list, you may wish to adopt it per se.

- Sp = spelling (ring the word)
- // = new paragraph here
- " " = speech marks here
- , = comma here
- ? = question mark here
- ! = exclamation mark here
- ' = apostrophe here
- Instead of individual punctuation marks, you may have P = punctuation error. This would be used by English teachers, because they would want the pupil to work out which punctuation mark should be used, rather than simply be shown.
- Gr = grammatical error
- Put a tick where they have made a good point
- Put a cross where they have made an error or used the wrong word; e.g. *'their'* instead of *'there'*.

In conclusion

- Mark regularly – little and often is best.
- Correct repeated errors rather than all errors.

Dos and Don'ts of Behaviour Management

- Try not to put a mark down.

- Praise pupils for their efforts.

- Drip-feed mark – do it as it comes in rather than waiting for a whole set to be done.

- Direct pupils to an area where they can improve.

- Give pupils time after you have marked work to go over it and learn from mistakes.

- Formative is always better than summative.

Do Not Negatively Label

This is fundamental to everything that you will encounter when dealing with pupils, and it goes very neatly with the section on the use of praise. You will hear pupils being labelled by other staff, and of course there are a plethora of labels that are employed. If the label is a positive one, then that is fine and should be encouraged. Sadly, that is a rarity; it is the poorly motivated and poorly self-disciplined pupils who often end up being labelled.

Eventually, the pupil becomes the label. If you tell a pupil often enough that he is a disruptive influence, he will surrender to the title and become it even more. If you tell a pupil that she is a naughty little girl who constantly makes life difficult for everyone, she will eventually become that even more. These are the very pupils we need to be positively affecting and we will not achieve that by sticking a label on them and reaffirming that label at every turn.

You will not change a pupil's attitude or behaviour if all you can do is to tell her/him that s/he is basically bad. Those pupils need to be told constantly that they are better than they are behaving and they need to be given structure, support, strategies for improvement and loads of praise for the most obvious or 'ordinary' things they do right.

Remember: one negative comment can undo a great deal of hard work and encouragement and set a pupil like this back a long way. And remember also that this pupil may be receiving such negative comments from a whole range of staff, and other adults, every day, and many times a day. You may not, as the solitary teacher, be able to significantly arrest that trend, but the pupil will respect you, and give you far less strife if s/he perceives you as someone who actually gives her/him a break from the rather dismal norm of every-day experience.

In terms of behaviour management of pupils, negative labelling is one of the top causes of already poorly behaved pupils continuing to be so and ultimately becoming worse.

The Use of Praise

Picture this scenario, which will be played out all too frequently across the country: it's a cold, dark morning and no-one is stirring in the house, except our pupil.

Dos and Don'ts of Behaviour Management

S/he is cold and does not really want to go to school, but s/he is going to anyway. Mam and Dad, if s/he is fortunate enough to have both, are in bed asleep and will remain there. S/he gets washed in cold water, has no breakfast and may even have a younger brother or sister to see to.

So, s/he forgets a part of her/his uniform, or is a bit late to school, or has left pen, pencil and books at home. The chances are that after making this real effort to make it into school, where s/he does not want to be anyway, s/he will receive her/his first telling off of the day. Hardly seems fair, does it? The day deteriorates for this pupil and, as a consequence, there appears either another attendance statistic, or a disaffected pupil in the class, a pupil who is more than likely going to become a major behaviour problem as well.

Much better for everyone concerned, is if the pupil is praised for getting into school in the first place and we address the other issues carefully and sensitively. I regularly thank my more disaffected pupils for wearing a tie or getting into school, or having a planner or equipment. It has a profound effect and would have an even more profound one if we all did it! This also cements my positive relationship with the pupils. They see me as reasonable. They see me as someone whom they respect and trust. They see me as a person to whom they can turn. And the outcome: even if I was just their form tutor and/or teacher, and not the person they know as the main instrument of the school's behaviour management, that would be exactly the same reaction towards me, as it is for all those staff, who adopt this positive attitude towards pupils.

Do not underestimate the power of praise. *You cannot over-praise!* And pupils like the one I have just described need ten times more praise than the total of put-downs or telling-offs they receive. There will not be many of you who will disagree when I tell you that this ratio is usually the other way round.

Praise list

Praise pupils for any or all of the following (this list is not exhaustive):

- Getting to school.
- Arriving at school/lessons on time.
- Having equipment (some or all).
- Listening.
- Paying attention.
- Entering a classroom sensibly.
- Attempting work.
- Making any attempt at anything.
- Putting her/his hand up.
- Walking not running.
- Talking not shouting.

Dos and Don'ts of Behaviour Management

+ Sitting not slouching.

+ Lining up properly.

+ Treating each other respectfully.

And when you do verbally praise, make sure everyone in the vicinity knows what it is you are praising. This reinforces what you want to happen. It sends constant positive signals to all the pupils. And, despite what they might say, all pupils like praise and none of them like being told off! It is a positive behaviour management tool and a huge motivational influence.
So:

+ 'Well done, Mary, for having your equipment today!'

+ 'Well done all of you for coming into the classroom so sensibly!'

+ 'I appreciate the effort you've made getting into school today, Gary!'

+ 'Thank you for putting your hand up, Robert; that's excellent!'

And so on . . .
It might seem contrived, but it works! Praise them sincerely and do not make it patronizing. It works even better once you have established a good relationship with the pupils and they truly value your opinion.

The Use of Rewards

Now what I am about to say is going to have some of you throw your hands up in horror! Some of you may want to fling this book into the nearest bin immediately. But bear with me whilst I explain. Rewards, per se, have no real, long-term effect! Schools have become institutions that are besotted with the idea that rewards are the key to motivating pupils and keeping them so. There is a belief that rewards will transform the behaviour of pupils. They do not! There is little evidence to suggest that this is the case, either in education or the wider world of work, where there has been a considerable amount of research done into the topic.

Think of yourself and your own experiences. Think of those times when you have won something, gained a promotion or received a certificate for some kind of achievement, and then think how long that elation lasted. There is little doubt that a reward has an immediate effect upon the recipient, but this does not last long; it is transient and the business of the day often supersedes that feeling of well-being. So I am not advocating abolishing rewards; I am counselling caution about their effect in the long run and the potential harm that reward systems can cause.

Here's something to consider: what about those pupils who do not get rewarded? How do you think they feel? I have sat through prize-giving ceremonies and observed the handful of pupils who never received one award in their five years at the school. I have spoken to them and sympathized with them. In short, not receiving anything had a disastrous effect upon them. Some of them simply gave up! What was worse is the fact that these pupils had to sit through ceremonies where large numbers of their peers were receiving awards, some more than one.

Again, think about your own experiences in, say, a job interview, especially if it was an internal appointment where you knew the other candidates very well. The person who gets appointed is on a high, but it doesn't last. The people who do not get appointed can harbour a grudge indefinitely. I can think of several such occasions myself, where I was so disappointed I sought a job elsewhere and never really felt the same again about the place. It is no different for pupils.

All schools have rewards and awards and I am counselling care and a sympathetic approach to that. However, you are also a teacher in a classroom and it may well be the school policy that you have to hand out merit cards or 'cause for praise' certificates, or a sticker or a stamp in pupils' planners. This is a difficult position to be in, and you need to be sensitive to it. Give everyone an award and you devalue the system. Be too selective and you will disenfranchise some of the pupils in your classes. And this soon leads on to disaffection and poor behaviour.

So what do we do? There is one way that an award or reward can be made to pupils, and that is privately by mail to their home. Many schools operate a system whereby pupils receive commendation letters home on a regular basis. By doing it this way, the individual pupil gets a little buzz and other pupils do not get to know about it and, therefore, cannot be adversely affected by it. Additionally, parents/carers are receiving positive feedback, which in turn is passed on to the pupil, who feels even better about the situation. Job done!

I must confess that I have always used rewards very sparingly. I believe that a genuine word of praise, a pleasant comment written or spoken about a piece of work, a word of appreciation for something a pupil has done, or a metaphorical (even physical!) pat on the back, is a much more cherished and a longer lasting 'reward' than many of the more artificially contrived ones. And I do write letters home to parents/carers, as just described. However, if you do throw your educational lot behind reward schemes, please be sensitive, sensible and aware of the potential pitfalls.

I hope you are still reading this book and it has not been consigned to the bottom of the bin!

PPA and More Essential Ingredients of a Good Lesson

I have already mentioned the importance of doing lesson plans; now I want to flesh that out and give you an insight into how to do them, and for that not to be too onerous or arduous a task. We now have Planning,

Dos and Don'ts of Behaviour Management

Preparation and Assessment (PPA) time, but one thing for certain is that it will not be long enough for you to do it all, but it is a step in the right direction. What you need, if you can remember what I said about the 6Ps at the beginning of this section, is to be well organized. This will lead to good planning and preparation and make you more economical with your time. As I have mentioned and will frequently point out: good, interesting lessons stand a much greater chance of success and a much reduced chance of pupil disruption taking place.

First, and very importantly, you must have access to a PC or laptop and you must be able to use it! It is inconceivable in this day and age for those basic premises not to be the case. Please, do not write lesson plans and schemes of work out by hand, because it means you are basically returning to square one with every lesson or scheme you put together. Take hard copies by all means; in fact it is essential: technology will eventually let you down and always when you either least expect or want it to! But, I beg you: do not see handwritten plans or schemes of work as the answer. They will cost you valuable time and effort.

So what do I do? Now, I must accept that I have a reduced timetable, but that only means it is even more important for you to follow this advice. Time spent in your first year of teaching your subject or subjects will reap massive dividends later on, because once you have your plans and schemes of work on disc, you can then tweak them to suit and resave them as another file. In this way, you will build a huge lesson plan database, as well as the files of work which will form the substance of your lessons.

The current theory is the three-part lesson plan. I know what they mean when they say that, but it is a potential banana skin. I am going to go out on a limb and disagree with it, especially if the group in front of you is disaffected and low ability – and when I say 'low ability', I am really referring to their literacy levels.

My normal lesson commences with a quick starter task for pupils to be doing as they enter classroom (not always possible when, like me, you are teaching in five different classrooms); the opening exposition is no more than five minutes; then I break the lesson up into three, four or five 'chunks', with a plenary at the end. In this way, you are in control of your lesson at all times in terms of the material and the substance.

However, you do need to be flexible. You may discover that one of the 'chunks' develops into something unforeseen and you may decide to explore this potential route. As you become more proficient and experienced, this will come naturally. The problem with the three-part lesson is that some teachers may well see the middle part between the exposition and the plenary as one task. There are precious few groups of pupils who can stay with the one task for that period of time. So, I might be accused here of being pedantic, but I did not want anyone to think that that was what constituted a three-part lesson.

Dos and Don'ts of Behaviour Management

I am extremely fortunate because we have interactive whiteboards in every classroom, and if I want the youngsters to do an exercise from a pre-prepared worksheet, all I have written down on my lesson plan is the name of the document, followed by how long it will take to do. Naturally this appears in chronological order in my plan. In this way, my lesson plans take a much shorter time to write up; I am clear what it is I am doing, when and for how long, and it saves on the photocopying bill. Now I accept that you will probably not find yourself in that situation, but the principle is the same. You will need worksheets to either hand out or write up on the board. Be careful if you are spending too much time with you back to pupils writing work on the board. However, you could use an overhead projector and acetate your worksheets. By structuring your lesson in this way, the lesson has a bounce and a flow to it; you can quickly move onto another aspect of the work if it is not going well and it allows you to drive the lesson.

I hope that will have given you an idea about how to plan and prepare. Now, what about the delivery of the lesson? The learning objective of each lesson must be made abundantly clear to the pupils. Indeed you should keep referring to this throughout the lesson. At the time of writing, and I say that advisedly, because if you are new into teaching, now is the time to become accustomed to the DCES and its obsession with the latest fad, OFSTED will observe your lesson for the quality of the *learning* which is taking place and *not* the teaching. To be candid, I strongly believe that they have actually got this one right. Teaching is an idiosyncratic skill and long may it be so. How you teach is never as important as how much the youngsters learn as a result of your teaching. With that in mind, repeated references to the learning objective is crucially important, and here's a tip: if an OFSTED inspector watches you teach, refer to what the pupils should be learning or should have learnt up to that point the second s/he enters the room and repeatedly do this until s/he leaves.

Idiosyncratic or not, how you engage the pupils is the key. Your exposition needs to be bouncy, interesting and challenging. This is the real high-energy part of your teaching in the lesson: grab them here and you will have a much-enhanced chance of keeping them. Get them involved in an actual task as soon as possible: make it short, snappy and something that they can succeed in; then they can self-assess which is germane to the overall objective of the lesson. I have found that nothing concentrates youngsters more than the short, sharp, accessible task.

So the PP has been sorted, and the A (Assessment) is catered for in the section 'Marking' earlier in this chapter. I will add here though that one of the new initiatives is AFL, or Assessment for Learning. No matter at what stage you are in your teaching career, you would be well advised to clue up in some detail on AFL and also put it into practice. In brief, it concerns itself with assessment being used as a positive tool for learning: the way in which we mark, how we mark, the kind of comments we put at the end of a piece of work and giving the pupils the necessary steps by which they can improve. There are some ideas on this at the end of the 'Marking' section. You will need to be prepared to take this on as one of those initiatives that has staying power, simply because it works and it makes good, sound, educational sense.

If you follow the advice above, you will have an extensive range of lesson plans and exercises and schemes of work by the end of your first year. If you are in a secondary school, these need to be shared by the staff in your department; the head of that department should be coordinating this. In this way you are networking and sharing good practice, and seriously cutting down on individual planning and preparation. One word of warning though: if it is not your lesson plan, do have a careful look over it and *make it your own* before you go into the classroom. If you are in a primary school, you will either be a particular year group teacher and you can use what you planned again (but always look to revise and improve), and if you are given a different year group to teach I can only hope that the head of the school has developed a similar system to the one described in a secondary school's department or faculty. Whichever system you happen to work in, you need to start working along-side your colleagues in a transparent and productive way. This will improve the quality of the lessons and the material you use; and it will reduce incidents of poor behaviour.

So:

PPA + A Well Structured, Interesting Lesson
= More Motivated, Successful and
Better Behaved Pupils

4 How to Successfully Build and Maintain Positive Relationships with Pupils

What I have attempted to do so far is to show you many of the pro-active, positive and successful things that you can do to produce situations where the vast majority of the pupils you teach are on your side. If you have followed my advice and put it into practice, you will already be in a situation where your potential problems with pupils have been considerably diminished. You have made the best possible start, and it is now imperative that we maintain and develop it.

Respect and Dignity

Behaviour management is not about punishment. It is not about reacting. It is not about confrontation. Most teachers who experience poor discipline have poor relationships with their pupils. Never forget that you have a major advantage over your charges: you are an adult and, as such, you are more experienced, more sophisticated and have developed a more highly attuned intellect, which you need to employ gainfully and sensitively. Use these facts to your advantage and never ever believe that youngsters have different feelings than you. They do not.

I said earlier on that the most important thing you take into any situation with youngsters is your confidence. I stand by that. However, the next two most important elements to being a successful teacher are respect and dignity. These two are the cornerstones of building positive, working relationships with youngsters. Disregard them at your peril!

When my two sons grew up and went to school, a transformation in the way I dealt with pupils came about. When you have your own children, you realize much more clearly how you want them to be treated by other adults. I began to consider how many youngsters' dignity I had destroyed by the way I had handled them and, how in so doing, had shown them scant respect. It was a sobering moment. In many ways I had bullied youngsters into submission. The worrying aspect to this is that I actually thought that I was good with youngsters and that what I was doing was right. I was wrong, and so is any other teacher who abuses their power and authority in this fashion.

This does not mean that there will not be occasions when you will have to be stern, raise your voice or

69

deliver an old-fashioned dressing down to an individual, a group, a class, a year group, or even a whole school! It is how you do it and what you do afterwards that really matter, as I shall endeavour to explain.

Every youngster has the right to be treated with respect and dignity. When we do this, we ourselves are acting as positive role models. We are much more likely to receive respect from the pupils if we show them respect in the first place. And remember, a very powerful argument to use with pupils is: 'I speak to you respectfully and politely. I expect the same from you.' Pupils are very quick to pick up on injustice and what they see and perceive as being unfair.

Developing this a little further, you need to be sure that you are treated with respect also.

Let me give an example:

You speak to a pupil and they respond with: 'What?' or 'Eh?' or something similar. Don't let this pass by without a comment. If you have spoken respectfully to that pupil – which you should have done – you can ask them to do the same. So my reply could be: 'I need you to answer me more respectfully. "Yes, Mr Dunn" is the proper way to respond. So we'll start again.' Repeat what you originally said to the pupil and wait for the response you have suggested. This is another example of coaching: you have modelled what you want the pupil to do and you then expect the pupil to do it. When they do it, thank them for doing so.

Build and Maintain Positive Relationships with Pupils

If the pupil continues to be uncooperative, you need to go through the procedure again. Remember: stay calm, don't be aggressive, and keep playing the same card about the fact that you are being respectful to them. Of course, if they still persist in being rude, you need to tell them that you are going to pass that fact on to a higher authority. If this happens, you should try and make the effort to be with that 'higher authority' when s/he talks to the pupil. I know that this is not always possible but, where and when it is, make sure you are there. It's even worthwhile asking the teacher to whom you have referred the pupil if they can arrange for you to be there when the pupil is spoken to.

If you wander around a school as I do as a part of my job, it is the odd remark made by a member of staff that jars and makes the wrong impression. Hearing a teacher shout: 'Shut up!' is one of those remarks. There is so much in this simple remark that is not good. For a starter, there is no respect being shown here by the teacher whatsoever; second, all it displays is that the teacher has lost control over that class; and third, believe me, the pupils in that class will know it too! Clichés become clichés because they are true and the saying 'If you can keep your head when all around are losing theirs' is very apposite to this situation. It takes control, but now is the chance to show these pupils that they have not got you on the run. If you can stay calm now and even talk quietly and respectfully to them, it will have a much better and more positive result than shouting at them.

Dos and Don'ts of Behaviour Management

So the scenario goes like this: you stand perfectly quiet and perfectly still. Make eye contact with as many pupils as you can and register real disapproval on your face. Then quietly say: 'I'm waiting. I need you to settle down.' (You will become very familiar with the 'I need' construct, and there is a whole chapter dedicated to it later on.)

Some will settle down, but you need to tough it out. Now a little firmer and just a little louder: 'I'm still waiting. I ... need ... you ... to settle down.' You are still very much in control, although I grant you that you will not be feeling like you are! A few more will settle down. Thank them for doing so. 'Thank you, you three; well done!' A useful example of how and where to use praise.

You now need to move towards those pupils who are still not doing as you asked. 'I have asked politely for you to settle down on two occasions.' (Firmly): 'Sit down, please and pay attention.' Thank them if they do.

If there are still pupils not responding, you need to issue a warning sanction and carry it out if they do not respond. So, I can hear you say: what if these strategies have little or no effect and you feel like exploding at them? Don't explode! Select one pupil who has settled down (there will inevitably be one) and send her/him to get another teacher. When the other teacher arrives, s/he should see you still apparently calm, not shouting, but quietly attempting to bring the class to order.

Now you might think that you have lost this particular battle, but let's look at the ramifications of this proposed action, as opposed to losing your control and losing your sense of respect and dignity for the pupils. If you lose your control and shout and even become quite aggressive, the pupils will glean the following:

♦ You can be pushed and you will break.

♦ You have little or no respect for them (you may well feel like you don't at moments like these!).

♦ You have little or no control.

♦ You are not someone to respect.

However, if you follow my advice, the chances are that they will glean the following from your actions and behaviour:

♦ You are a calm customer.

♦ You don't panic.

♦ You respect them despite their poor behaviour.

♦ You are someone who should be respected in turn (maybe not immediately, but you need to work on this with that particular group).

And the next time you see them, you need to register disapproval and disappointment at the way that certain individuals behaved. You also need to warmly thank those who listened to you. If you can continue in this vein, you will experience a much better relationship with those pupils and a mutual respect will form. It will not happen immediately, but if you do not maintain respect and dignity, it will never occur!

No Room for Sarcasm

They say that sarcasm is the lowest form of wit, and this has become a cliché as well used as the football manager 'taking each game as it comes'! In a school situation, sarcasm employed by teachers can be the most destructive of strategies to adopt when dealing with pupils. Sarcasm not only strips away respect and dignity, it also introduces other elements as well, like belittling, mocking and showing a person up in front of her/his peers. You will rarely be forgiven if you do it and the potential backlash is really not worth it.

So why do staff resort to sarcasm? It's understandable, because there are times when a teacher can feel that there is just no other way of dealing with a situation than to personally vilify and verbally destroy the person in front of her/him. I talk about the amygdala response later, where your emotions take over your intellect (and pupils will notice this). But all too often sarcasm does not fit into this category. It is a cold and deliberate form of talking, and pupils will see it as such and will quickly come to dislike you. Of the staff I have to field complaints about in school, the vast majority of them fall into this category. The pupils just do not like or respect them, because the teachers do not treat them with respect. It is a simple equation to work out.

Firm and Fair

The golden motto must always be: 'Firm and Fair'. You cannot afford not to be firm when the occasion arises, but you must always be fair and even-handed in the way that you deal with situations. Three words should always be used by teachers in almost every situation: 'Please' and 'Thank You'. This is another good habit and should be adopted so that it becomes second nature to you. When you ask a class to go into a room, put 'Please' at the end of the instruction and then add 'Thank you' when they do it. In this way you are inculcating good manners and just as importantly showing respect for your charges. The other benefit is that you are introducing praise into your teaching, even for them doing that which is expected.

Even if sometimes when I am engaged in managing pupils on the corridor or involved in crowd control out in the yard, I need to raise my voice and be abrupt in my instructions, I still put 'please' and 'thank you' into the equation. Again, this means I can always say to them that I have asked them to do something respectfully. It is a very persuasive argument.

So what happens if you ignore my advice? What happens when you strip pupils' dignity away from them and show them little or no respect? The answer is simple: they will reciprocate in kind and, believe me, it will often be reciprocated in spades! Or, they will retire into their shell and refuse to respond to you as their teacher. They will deliberately under-perform. I am sure that you can think of those teachers for whom you refused to work. Sadly, like pupils now, you probably thought you were teaching that teacher a lesson! Instead, your education suffered, as will that of those pupils you treat in this way.

This, however, does not mean that you have to simply put up with their poor behaviour, rudeness and refusal to follow instructions. Certainly not! And here is how you do it.

There will always be pupils who are disaffected and really do not want to be in school. There will be others who find it difficult to behave for a whole host of reasons, some medical, some psychological, some ingrained by environmental and home conditions. If these pupils are not checked, anarchy will rule in your classroom. You are the boss and it is you who sets the example and decides what is and is not acceptable in your classroom.

One thing that I have always found to be the case in teaching is that pupils actually like order and control and discipline, and, equally, they like those teachers who provide that much more than those who do not. Pupils are no different to anyone else: they basically like security and therefore respond much more favourably to teachers who are capable of providing it. Pupils also need consistency. Too often I see teachers being inconsistent in the way that they deal with youngsters. Sometimes this is brought about by stress, but too often it is simply down to either inexperience or a disregard for the feelings of a young person.

'Do unto others as you would have them do unto you.' This is a very useful 'watch-phrase' for those in the teaching profession. We have all been on the end of a telling-off or a dressing down. Think how you felt at the end of that and how you felt about the way it had been done. Did you feel that you had been treated with respect and/or dignity? Did you feel that you had been treated fairly? Did you feel that you were given an opportunity to explain your side of events? Were you turned off by the experience? How did you feel about the person who had delivered the telling-off? Believe me when I tell you that youngsters have exactly the same feelings as we do, but with one vital exception: they do not possess the maturity, sophistication and life experience which allow us to handle it as effectively. So for them, this can lead to an irrevocable breakdown in their relationships with those teachers who have treated them in this way. And, let's face it: that may have been the outcome for you as well when you were a pupil! Think about it before you make the same mistake.

I'll be perfectly candid here: I sometimes have to take a member of staff to one side and have 'words' with her/him. I do not personally see this as something I should, by definition, handle significantly differently to how I deal with the vast majority of pupils. The point I am making here is that we should be adopting the same approach, irrespective of age, and this should be done respectfully and sensitively.

Hands Up – I Was Wrong!

A part of showing respect and dignity is sometimes being able to accept that you are wrong. Pupils, as I have mentioned, have just as keen a sense of fair play and injustice as any adult. If you make a mistake, don't be frightened to put your hand up and admit to it. It is not unusual for a teacher to blame a pupil for a particular act, only to discover that s/he was not actually to blame. Simply say: 'I am sorry, I got that wrong; my apologies.' It does not need anymore than that and it will stand you in far better shape than you either not apologizing or trying to bluff it out.

Remember, pupils have their opinions, their thoughts and their feelings: always be prepared both to listen and to let them know that you are prepared to listen. You can always turn this around to your advantage in future exchanges by pointing out that schools are about education in the broadest of terms, not just passing examinations (this is very important for those pupils who are not going to succeed academically). That means we can learn from our mistakes, but to do that we have to own up to them first. Inculcating the notion that honesty is always the best policy is crucially important. Besides, once again, you are being the role model.

Let me give some real examples of how teachers can get it wrong.

Example A (This is so common it is unreal!) The teacher is otherwise engaged with another pupil, maybe checking work or helping. S/he becomes aware of someone talking and makes an instant decision about who is the culprit. However, the teacher has got it wrong. Not only is s/he wrong, but s/he compounds the problem by ending up in an argument with the pupil, who is rightly indignant and starts to fight her/his corner. This is now beginning to escalate out of control.

What should we do? First, and obviously, be very careful before you accuse a pupil of doing something, especially if you are not 100 per cent sure. And then, even if you are, be equally careful about the way you go about bringing the pupil to task. Be more general rather than specific. So, instead of singling out the pupil you 'think' has transgressed, say: 'Someone in that group is talking and I need that person to get on with her/his work.'

This is much better, because it prevents a potential mistake being made; it does not single anyone in particular out; it draws attention to the fact that you as the teacher are aware of someone talking; and it also allows the pupil who is talking to quietly merge back into the background, without any more attention being drawn to her/him. Potentially, everyone is a winner doing it this way and you have avoided that dreaded confrontation where the pupil denies it was her/him and an educational Mexican stand-off occurs, with the possible outcome of you wrongly accusing someone and feeling that you cannot go back on this, and the pupil rightly feeling aggrieved. If you find yourself in this predicament, you need to say something like: 'I may have got it wrong this time and if it wasn't you, Gary, I apologize. However, someone is talking over there and I need it to stop.' Gary will almost certainly accept this whether he was 'guilty' or not. And if the teacher does not follow this course of action, you should know by now that the pupil is going to harbour resentment towards you.

Example B The teacher observes an incident, which s/he believes to be a deliberate act on the part of the pupil, but it is actually an accident. Let's say a window is broken by a pupil, Gary, who has been throwing small stones at a wall. One has hit the window by accident and this has been seen by the teacher. When I say 'seen', what I am actually saying is seen in a single moment in time, which then plays out in the teacher's mind as a whole episode, making the teacher sure that Gary carried out the act deliberately. Think how many times referees get important decisions wrong in a football match. Like them, we do not have the benefit of slow-motion action replay.

What not to do is to become accusatory from the outset. Remember that what we have just 'witnessed' may be a total accident on behalf of the pupil. So ask, don't tell! Do not wade in and start accusing Gary of deliberately breaking the window and then frogmarch him to the nearest senior member of staff for his just desserts. Be a little more patient, a little more reflective and give yourself some breathing space, just to make sure.

So:

Teacher: 'Gary, can you explain what's just happened?' (You have probably gathered that our Gary is a bit of a pain by now!)

Gary: 'It wasn't me!' (You'll be amazed how often pupils say this!)

Teacher: 'It wasn't you who did what?'

Gary: 'Smashed the window.'

Teacher: 'So I didn't see you throw that stone at the window?'

This will generally confuse a pupil because s/he knows the game is up to a certain extent, and you are putting the onus on her/him to come clean. What can happen now is that the pupil explains what happened and why. Yes, the window is still broken, but there may not have been intent to cause that damage.

Teacher: 'Why did you throw the stone at the window?'

Here, you are giving Gary the chance to explain and, at the same time, you are closing down any thought in his mind that you do not know that he is responsible for that action. What you are not doing, however, is making your mind up about the motives behind the incident, which is vitally important.

It is much better to have taken the time to handle the situation in this manner, than to once again face a possibly distraught pupil who will end up resenting how s/he has been treated. If you have adopted an accusatory tone from the outset and it becomes clear as you investigate that you are wrong, apologize: 'OK, Gary, you've convinced me it was an accident. I'm sorry that I thought you did it deliberately. However, [always try and throw in an 'educational angle'] it was a silly thing to do and I hope you have learned from the experience.'

Better, though, not to get to the point where the apology is necessary.

The Disappointment Card

I hope that by now your relationship with your pupils is good and based on mutual trust and respect. It is vital that it should be so. You have built that up, you have made it so and now you can really use it to full effect.

There is another omnipotent and rewarding way of registering disapproval whilst also maintaining respect and dignity, and that is to play the most valuable card in your deck: the disappointment card. Success in the classroom eventually comes down to the one thing that I have been stressing from the outset of this book: positive relationships. Never underestimate the effect that you will be having on the pupils in front of you. I have known pupils who have given a particular teacher real strife, only to be devastated when they discover that the teacher is leaving. It is a strange phenomenon, but one well known to the supply teacher: youngsters prefer their everyday teacher(s) to the one who suddenly appears in front of them as the substitute (unless of course, that substitute teacher is dynamic and well organized). And all teachers can use this relationship to their immediate advantage. When a pupil does something that makes you need to reprimand them, try this line: 'Mary, I am very disappointed in you. I thought you were better than that!'

This line, which is one you really need to employ commonly, is a very important one to use. It is very powerful, because it makes pupils think; it makes them feel valued by you; and it gives them the opportunity to show you that they can behave better next time or in the future. Use this particular construction time and again.

This is extremely powerful even if you do not feel that you are getting the desired response immediately. It functions on several levels. It works on the relationship level, because the pupil will value your opinion, and the vast majority of pupils want you to have a good opinion of them. It works on the value level also, because it implies that you think highly of her/him but s/he has erred on this occasion. And finally it works on the respect and dignity level: you have registered your disapproval in a quiet, calm, yet respectful and digni-fied way. The pupil has been given the opportunity to respond positively without feeling that s/he has been shown up in front of her/his peers.

Examples:

♦ 'Mary, I am really disappointed in your attitude this lesson. I feel really let down by you. I know you can work a lot better than this and I can't believe what I have seen today.'

♦ 'Robert, I am disappointed that I have had to single you out and speak to you. This is not what I expect from you, because I know you are better than this. I feel personally badly let down by you.'

♦ 'I can't believe that you have been involved in this incident, Gary. I am bitterly disappointed with you on a personal level. I expect a lot more from you than this.'

♦ 'I have a great deal of respect for you, Robert, and have always found you to be a responsible pupil. I am shocked that you can behave in this way.'

♦ 'I have always enjoyed a good relationship with you, Mary and I am really upset that this has happened.'

Build and Maintain Positive Relationships with Pupils

All of the above will work superbly if you have developed a strong relationship with a pupil. Even if you have not, using this particular strategy will still have her/him thinking about the relationship between the two of you, and might well go a long way to improve it. Either way, it sends strong messages to the pupil that you disapprove of what s/he has done, and that you feel let down because you believe her/him to be a lot better than the way in which s/he has behaved. All very powerful!

The Positive Use of Humour, Empathy and Common Sense

One of the major ingredients you will need to possess if you want to be a successful teacher is a good sense of humour. This is as apparent in the staffroom with your colleagues as it is when you actually have to deal with situations in the classroom and out on the corridors and playgrounds. I will consistently make a great deal out of trying to avoid confrontations and on how to avoid escalating situations. I will also repeatedly emphasize the point that youngsters are basically just younger versions of ourselves; if we constantly employ empathy and common sense in our thinking and our strategies, we will not go far wrong.

Of course, the big difference between ourselves and our young charges is their lack of life experience and their lack of sophistication. Much that they do is about experiencing things from a more naïve perspective.

Dos and Don'ts of Behaviour Management

There are a number of advertisements on the television trying to tempt people into the teaching profession. I cannot say any of them have touched base with me personally or, for that matter, with any of my friends and colleagues in the profession. However, one comment from one of these advertisements about the fact that youngsters are unpredictable does resonate. Because they are! That can be a factor that can throw you off balance at times, but if you can just maintain some semblance of equilibrium and proportion, you can very readily turn it to your own advantage.

The learned response

Let us take swearing: it is something that most teachers will not tolerate, and as educationalists we should be encouraging better use of language. However, for many youngsters swearing is very much a learned and honed way of communicating and, outside of the school environment, one that they may use more often than not. If we push a youngster too much, we are simply going to invoke a learned response from them, which is for them to swear at us.

So what is this 'learned response' and how does being aware of it assist us in our management of people? Psychologists will tell you that the brain in all its complexity is capable of almost anything, but that it can be conditioned and, as a result, can be predictable. Our environment, the influencing factors within it and the way in which we have been brought up are key factors in determining a number of these more predictable moments in people.

A learned response is, as the phrase suggests, a reaction to a given stimulus or stimuli that has been inculcated into the person over time, and generally from a very young age when a person is most receptive. None of us are immune from this: action A occurs and the response will be reaction B: the learned response. As we mature and become, we hope, more sophisticated and more aware, so we can appreciate what our own learned responses are and begin to counteract them actively. This is not an easy thing to accomplish, but it is not impossible. However, youngsters in our schools are very much more prone to reacting in these learned fashions and we need to be able to both understand that and to be proactive in our dealings with them.

Let me give some examples of learned responses. The first is the one I have just mentioned above which is swearing. Where have people learned to swear? Well not in your lessons! They have learned this in their immediate surroundings, often their home situation. I meet parents every day as part of my job and it does not take long to recognize how a particular youngster has turned out the way s/he has. If the parent swears and it is commonplace in the home, the likelihood of the children from that household swearing is almost certain. What is more, because swearing is often used at times of high emotion between these family

Dos and Don'ts of Behaviour Management

members, it is not too difficult to see how a pupil in your school would resort to it in certain situations. You need to be aware of this. In every school in which I have taught, a pupil swearing at a member of staff almost always means the pupil will be referred to someone in authority and this often leads to an exclusion. So what is the learning going on here? Yes, the pupil has been excluded and is aware of the reason why; but are we not charged with doing more than that, such as attempting to prevent the situation occurring in the first place, which is what being aware of learned responses might just bring about?

One of the most difficult learned responses to manage is the one that manifests itself in a total refusal to cooperate. I would have to say that it is this type of behaviour that is probably the most complicated and most time-consuming to handle. It usually comes about when a youngster feels wronged, picked on or victimized, often by a teacher or another adult. It results in shut down on the pupil's part and a total refusal to communicate or cooperate. In practically every one of these instances, the person who has produced this response will not be the one who will be able to bring the pupil out of it. So remember: if you have elicited this response in the pupil, you will almost certainly need to seek assistance from someone else to resolve it. You will also need to build the bridge with that pupil afterwards at a more opportune moment when s/he has calmed down.

Build and Maintain Positive Relationships with Pupils

I am certainly not immune from creating such responses, but I do quickly learn and work out what brought the response about in the first place and determine not to repeat that way of handling the pupil in future. Additionally, I add it to my bank of experiences, upon which I draw to make me think a little more closely about whether my approach to the pupil who responded unfavourably is also one that I need to be wary of using with other youngsters, whom I might consider in a similar category. This is not a simple categorization of pupils, but rather being more aware of the potential for creating a situation which you cannot then control. In short: what I did brought about that response! What have I learned from it? Will it modify the way I act in future? For many teachers that, sadly, is not the case: they make the same mistakes time and again, often with the same pupils. Do not become one of them!

So, a forewarned, common sense, empathetic approach to young people is the answer. It is imperative that teachers know their charges well and, if they do not, more fool them. This knowledge and understanding of the way people react will help teachers not to make repeated mistakes of pressing the wrong buttons at the wrong times with the wrong pupils, resulting in a series of learned responses often causing aggressive, abusive responses from the youngsters. It is far better to deal with situations tactically and calmly, in a measured and tolerant way, especially with youngsters who have something of a history for this kind of

Dos and Don'ts of Behaviour Management

reaction. Remember that you should have an up-to-date special needs register for each of your classes.

Common situations

Moving away from learned responses, here is another typical school scenario: two pupils running down the corridor, one of them chasing the other. We can shout at them, upbraid them and send them on their way with the proverbial flea in their ear, which may mean that they turn up to their next lesson in a less than positive frame of mind. Or, we can use common sense and a little bit of humour. You see the pair and stand and block their way and raise your hands at the same time. You smile (puts them at ease because they are not threatened by you) and say, 'Whoa!' or something similar, but nothing too heavy though. Then I often ask them this: 'Are you going to my lesson now?' They are not and so they naturally answer in the negative. To which I reply: 'Well, I can't see why you're rushing! I could understand it if you were mad keen to be taught by me!' They have been stopped, they have had a few seconds to calm down, they may even smile at your attempt at humour; you are now in a position to have a quiet word about the potential hazards of running around a corridor. Tell them that you expect more common sense from them and then let them go. In this way, with any luck, they will have learnt something and they will not be in a negative or upset frame of mind when they get to their next lesson. Doing this once will have a limited effect: everyone in the school doing it repeatedly and consistently will: it is all about inculcation. We can achieve better success if we can elicit a positive response from the youngsters.

Do not ever forget that how you treat pupils has a knock-on effect in the way they will behave for their next teacher. If you have been a teacher for a while, you will be all too aware of the times when a youngster arrives at your lesson in a foul mood because of the way s/he has been dealt with by one of your colleagues a few minutes earlier. Common sense and empathy for your fellow colleagues are so important.

Here is another scenario, and we're back to swearing again: you hear a pupil swearing at another pupil. You were not meant to hear the swearing, but you did. You can do one of two things: pretend you didn't hear, or do something about it. The only time I would advocate the first option is if you believe yourself to be in a real lose/lose situation. You have quickly assessed where you are, who the pupils are and take the pragmatic decision that the best course of action is not to take action. If you do find yourself in this predicament, my advice is to make eye contact, shake your head with pursed lips and with a 'tut tut' walk away. At least you have registered disapproval and not put yourself in a position from which you might have come out on the losing side.

But fortunately, you are not in this position and you decide that action is required. Again, you have choices.

Dos and Don'ts of Behaviour Management

Do you wade in and issue stern warnings, report them for their bad language, or do you adopt a more pragmatic and common sense approach? Remember, you were not meant to hear them swearing. One approach I use is to cough melodramatically, grimace when they look over and cover my ears with my hands. Remember the disappointment card? Use it here. Register your disapproval in a way that suggests to the pupil or pupils that you thought that they were better than this. Then walk away! Do not prolong it. You have registered your disapproval and indicated what you expect in future, so now move on.

Naturally, if you catch this pupil in the same situation again, you may need to issue a warning and contemplate passing it on to a Head of Year or someone similar to have further words with her/him. But certainly as an initial encounter, the first method is much more likely to achieve the desired effect, especially if the pupil respects the way that you have handled the situation and the way in which you have not over-reacted to what s/he has done.

Humour is a little bit like beauty, in that it lies in the eye of the beholder. However, as a teacher, you do not need to be on a par with a stand-up comedian; rather, you are using humour to diffuse and dilute potentially explosive situations. Youngsters respond very positively to teachers who employ humour, because it immediately sets them at ease, reduces friction and tension and establishes the opportunity for productive relationships. Even the most disaffected pupils respond to a teacher who can make a lesson 'entertaining' and therefore engender genuine interest. They can balance the positive effect this has on them with the downside that they may not be very good at that particular lesson. They will also, without doubt, start to improve.

This is not just about 'having a laugh; it is about being able to relax. And when you do, let us consider the signals that this sends to your pupils: you are confident in your ability; you are in control; you want them to enjoy your lessons; you obviously are considerate of their feelings. And, just as importantly, you will be seen as a person for whom they are likely to try harder and, naturally, behave better. If you have any doubt about what I am saying, just think back to the teachers who taught you. Who were the ones you identified with? Which teachers brought the best out of you? It will be the same for you as it is for the youngsters who are now in your charge.

Rules or Expectations

Schools have an abundance of rules: too many, and far too many that are very difficult to actually enforce. Let me give you some classic examples of the kind of rules I am referring to that I have encountered over the years:

- an access and/or exit door denied to pupils
- ties
- shirts

Dos and Don'ts of Behaviour Management

◆ shoes/trainers

◆ one-way systems

◆ equipment

◆ planners

◆ late-comers

Any of these familiar to you? Most secondary schools have a school uniform which is difficult to 'police' and maintain, especially if your school is situated in an area of social deprivation. But we still try our best to maintain 'standards' and teachers get very agitated and aerated when pupils fail to abide by the school's rules. In fact I have known situations in staff meetings where the above concerns have been the major issues rather than the quality of the learning that is taking place in the school, and this is because we have an innate feeling that these rules must be absolute. Of course, the major problem is: what do we do when the pupils 'break' these rules?

This could be a difficult one for you as an individual teacher, especially if you are new to the profession as well. It may well be that the school expects you to see to it that all pupils adhere rigidly to the rules. One of the rules could well be about equipment to lessons and that *all* pupils should be suitably equipped with pen, pencil, rubber and planner. I have already made it clear that I always take in a supply of pens for those who do not have one; I do not make an issue over it. I have also outlined what I suggest you do with late-comers: see Chapter 3.

You need to ask yourself a simple question: do I risk the success of a lesson by being a slave to school rules? However, be careful: your behaviour management policy may suggest that you should, in which case you might like the person(s) responsible for its creation to read this book!

Rules can make fools of schools

This is my spin on school rules. I prefer to talk about expectations rather than rules. In this way, you can have a much more meaningful dialogue with a youngster when s/he fails to meet that expectation. You are also turning it into an educational discussion and avoiding damaging confrontation. The other essential point to remember here is that you need to have a good reason for why you expect a pupil to do something. It is no good as I have mentioned elsewhere in this book, saying: 'Because I told you so!' or 'Because it is a school rule!'

You will always be able to stand a better chance of success if you are a role model. Teachers who arrive late to school themselves are hardly in the most advantageous position to talk to a pupil about her/his lateness. Teachers who frequently arrive to lessons late similarly put themselves in a questionable position. If I am late to a lesson, I will always apologize to the pupils and explain why I am late. You are that positive role model in all that you do, say and project. When I ask a pupil to put her/his tie up, mine already is. When I ask them to put their shirts in, mine already is. I expect them to walk on the left-hand side of the corridors and I do the same. You might be amazed at how many teachers actually do not! When I ask them where pupils' planners are, I can show them mine. Except in extreme weather conditions, I have never been late. In fact, I am an early bird and generally in school an hour before it officially starts. I can tell them this and use it. So when a pupil breaks the rules or, as I prefer to see it, does not meet expectations, we need to talk to them using a whole different approach, with the likelihood of a whole different and more positive response. Instead of seeing the situation as a person who is deliberately a rule-breaker, and therefore standing a very good chance of remonstrating with that person in that way, I hope you can now see that we can use this as an educational opportunity.

So how might we actually put this into practice and how do we actually speak to a pupil on this occasion? Let us take the case of a girl we will call Mary. She falls foul of just about every 'rule' the school has to offer! She is frequently late to school and late to her lessons, often wears trainers instead of shoes, either does not have a tie on or it is halfway down her front and is rarely seen with any equipment. Many of you who are practising teachers will be able to list the pupils in your school who remind you of Mary. That Mary so completely destroys everything that our rule-makers want to bring about, should probably tell you something about her in the first place: her home life, her aspirations, her self-esteem, her values, her attitude to school and learning. Simply laying into Mary, or those like her, is not the answer, because it will not work. Punishing her will only deepen her already poor attitude to school and make turning her into a more positive pupil impossible. Mary needs to be coaxed, cajoled, brought into the fold by much more persuasive means than those all too often employed in schools.

First, and I really need to emphasize this, it is not the duty of every member of staff who comes across Mary to have their individual 'digs'. This will be disastrous and only serve to drive a huge wedge between the school and the pupil. It needs to be the remit of one or two designated members of staff. And please, whilst I am on the topic, do not be a teacher who spends valuable teaching time on dressing-down pupils every lesson for any of the above misdemeanours.

Mary needs to be the recipient of a series of conversations which might go like this:

'Mary, I need to have a little chat with you.'

Now, take her away from her peers. This is a private chat, and she does not want or need to be publicly spoken to.

Dos and Don'ts of Behaviour Management

'Why do you think we need you to get to school on time?'

This immediately puts the onus on the pupil to start thinking about the situation. This is much more likely to achieve success than simply telling them. Be prepared to wait for an answer and tell her/him before you start that 'I don't know' or 'I dunno' is not an option for an answer. Tease a response by making suggestions about how you would like the question answered. When you get the response you want, re-enforce it and thank her/him for it. Do not do this patronizingly.

In this way you are entering into a much more meaningful dialogue with the pupil; you are engaging her/him on a personal and sympathetic level; you are developing trusting and strong relationships with the pupil and, finally, you are more likely to achieve the desired result. Finally, and very importantly, when you have had your conversation with the pupil, you need to set some targets that s/he can meet and which you 'expect' them to meet.

'Right, Mary, thank you for your cooperation; that's been a useful chat. Now, I need you to come to school on time every day and, just to make sure you do, you will report to (mention place) each morning at (mention time) to me for a week. OK?'

Do not go for every 'rule' that Mary is breaking. Start with the most important and build up in stages and do not be too disappointed if this is an exercise that you need to repeat on more than one occasion with her! Rome wasn't built in a day and Mary is not for changing in a day either!

So how does this tie in with behaviour management per se? It is an essential element simply because it allows you to adopt a more reasonable and more reasoned stance with pupils and they will recognize this. They will be especially appreciative if you are consistent in your approach; in this way you are doing what all successful teachers do: establishing strong, positive and productive relationships with your charges. We are back to respect and dignity. And remember too the empathy aspect: if someone had to speak to you about being late, how would you like it to be handled? I imagine it would be in a manner similar to the suggestions above about how you handle your pupils.

5 How to Handle Particularly Challenging Pupils

I sincerely hope that you understand why I have laid out my advice to you in the order I have. I cannot stress more stringently to you the need to be pro-active rather than reactive. The Six Ps and all that I have advised since then have all been about that. With all of that knowledge hopefully now put into practice, you are a well-equipped, well-organized, well-focused teacher, who has developed meaningful (and lasting) relationships in a remarkably short time, sometimes as short as a half term. However – and there sadly has to be a however – it will not make you immune to poor behaviour from some of the pupils who you are going to encounter, both in and out of the classroom. And remember: you do not teach every pupil in the school. You will not have had the opportunity to forge strong relationships with more than those pupils you actually teach. The good news is that your reputation will have been made and other pupils will know about it, because news travels.

So we now need to look at how we manage those pupils who refuse to comply, despite all that you have already pro-actively done.

'I' not 'You'

You will be realizing that there is a thread and a commonality of approach in the way that I handle pupils. But, as I am quite sure you will also realize, there will come a time when you will have to discipline, and you will have to impose sanctions, and these will occasionally mean that you have to remove a pupil or pupils from your classroom. Recall what I have already said? The first thing to do is to keep your own dignity, no matter what the provocation. I am generalizing now (I shall go into greater detail later), but keep your voice even, make your words very clear, be firm and, most importantly, put your instruction into the first person 'I'. Do not use the second person 'You'. If you look back at all the examples I have used up to now, you will see that this is common to them all. I have always used 'I' and never 'You'.

Believe me when I say that this will not come easily to you. I was intrigued when one of my newly qualified teachers came to see me to tell me that she had been practising this 'I' not 'You' technique on her own

Dos and Don'ts of Behaviour Management

children at home and that it had had a profound effect. I was very impressed, because it is not a natural construction for us to employ. As a teacher, we too often see ourselves in an authoritarian and autocratic way, and this psychologically affects not only the language we use, but also the construction of our sentences and the emphasis we place on certain words. We can undo much of the good work we have already achieved with ill thought out commands and instructions to pupils!

So, look at the three examples below. Think about what I have just said and ally that to everything you have read about respect, dignity and maintaining good relationships.

You are trying to get an awkward pupil (yes, it's Gary again!) to settle down to his work.

Example A: 'I need you to get on with your work, Gary.'

Example B: 'Get on with your work!'

Example C: 'Will you get on with your work?'

It could be even worse:

Example D: 'Shut up and get on with your work!'

Example A is respectful and authoritative at the same time. The use of 'I' is very powerful: it gives you authority and it puts you in charge, and psychologically it is sending that message to the pupil.

Example B is aggressive, lacks respect and is confrontational. It is not likely to succeed unless you are seen as an established power figure in the eyes of the pupil. There is every chance that this kind of remark could easily spark a confrontation, especially with a disaffected pupil and certainly with a pupil looking for an excuse to be troublesome.

Example C is nearly the worst of the three and is all too often used. It is weak and indecisive. It hands power to the pupil. So never put an instruction into question form, because it begs a negative response: 'Will you get on with your work, Gary?' Gary replies: 'No!' I am sure you can see that this is not a desirable situation to find yourself in. You are now on the back foot. What is more, what should have been a quiet word between you and the pupil is now in the public domain: the whole class will be taking a keen interest in what is going on and, more precisely, in what you are going to do about the situation. Even worse, the pupil who has given you the negative response may well now be up for the confrontation; after all he is on centre court with an audience! You have escalated an everyday lesson situation into a major confrontation.

Example D will simply destroy any relationship that you may have built up with that pupil and it also runs the risk of offending other pupils too. Do not be surprised that well-behaved and obliging pupils can get offended by the way their peers are treated, even those they recognize as the badly behaved ones. This kind of outburst is all too likely to backfire on you.

Let us look more closely at why we should not use the word 'You'. 'You' immediately disregards dignity and respect. For one, the pupil is nameless. There is no engagement with the pupil and it dilutes your authority, because while what you want to do is stress 'your' position as the person in charge of the situation, the use of 'you' stresses the pupil instead. The best way to put you in charge in these situations is by always using the word 'I', either at the beginning of each sentence, or straight after the name of the pupil who you are addressing.

Vary it:

'I would like you to get on with your work, Gary, please.'

'Gary, I would like you to get on with your work please.'

'I want you to get on with your work, Gary.'

'Gary, I want you to get on with your work.'

'I know it will be a lot better if you get on with your work, Gary.'

'Gary, I know it will be a lot better if you get on with your work.'

Notice that in each of these possibilities, 'I' or the pupil's name starts the sentence, and that where we have started with 'I', the name of the pupil is still used in the instruction. This sends a strong subliminal message to the pupil: that it is you in control and not him!

Consequences

There is no magic wand here. Just because you have used this construction does not guarantee success. So what do you do next if the pupil still refuses to follow your instruction? Repeat the instruction again, looking the pupil straight in the eyes. Make sure you are not too close – an arm's length is the closest you want to be – and if the pupil still refuses, tell her/him what will happen if s/he still continues to misbehave. You need to have a consequence for her/his defiance.

So the scenario could go like this:

A pupil (Robert this time – Gary has been sent from the room long ago!) is disrupting others around about him and not getting on with the task at hand. You call out the pupil's name (if it is a new class you have already worked out a seating plan, so a quick glance at it will give you her or his name). You do not walk towards the pupil, but deliver your first line from where you are.

'Robert.' (This gains his attention.) 'I need you to get on quietly with your work, Robert, please.'

He does not respond.

You walk up to him, staying at least an arm's length distance away.

Slowly, firmly and more quietly:

Dos and Don'ts of Behaviour Management

'I ... need ... you to get on with your work, Robert.' (No 'please' this time.) 'I have already asked you politely to do so and I expect you to follow my instruction.'

He still does not respond.

'I am going to ask you one more time Robert. If you do not follow this instruction, I will be forced to [name the sanction].'

If he responds:

'Thank you, Robert.'

If he does not respond:

Carry out the sanction. You must do this. Never make a threat you are not prepared to carry out.

If he does not respond to the sanction imposed by you:

Send another pupil to get another teacher to assist you, preferably one who you know will be able to cope with the pupil in question.

I mentioned that you should not get closer than an arm's length to a potentially troublesome pupil. The reasons for this are as follows: it is rude and aggressive to invade someone else's space (you don't like it and neither do they); and it can bring about a number of negative responses from a pupil: an emotional outburst, a verbal outburst or, worst of all, the potential for a physical outburst. Nothing in teaching distresses me more than seeing a pupil being shouted at by a teacher, literally a centimetre from her/his face. It is simply a form of bullying that should not be tolerated. We as staff hate it when we see pupils do it to each other: so why do we do it ourselves? And please tell me where is the respect and dignity in doing such a thing?

The Use of Your Body and the 90-Second Rule

Head to head confrontation is something that teachers are well advised to avoid. Too often teachers come off second best, and in your early days in the classroom this will almost certainly be the case. The trick is to avoid the confrontation sought-for by the pupil, but still come out as the person in charge. Additionally, you can do this with dignity and allow pupils to maintain theirs as well.

If a pupil is constantly causing a distraction or being disruptive, and your repeated verbal requests are falling on deaf ears, the use of your body and the subsequent 90-second talk you deliver to the rest of the class is an extremely powerful weapon to have in your educational arsenal. This is a precursor to you thinking about having to employ a sanction for their misbehaviour.

Dos and Don'ts of Behaviour Management

Go over to the pupil – remember: not too close – and speak firmly and directly to her/him using the 'I need' format. Do not allow her/him time to respond. Turn your back to her/him and engage the rest of the class in a 90-second (not exact time!) 'talk' on anything at all: the work they are currently doing, what you need them still to do, the weather, last night's football – anything at all! At the conclusion of your 'talk', tell them all to return to what they were doing, give the miscreant a quick look and say 'Thank you' if they are now quiet and behaving.

This tactic works on five different levels:

+ You retain control.

+ You have demonstrated that to the whole class.

+ By the use of your body, you have 'separated' the miscreant from the rest of the class – this is very meaningful, because you have disenfranchized this pupil and taken away her/his power.

+ You have given the miscreant a period of time (approximately 90 seconds) to exorcize any anger or resentment s/he may feel.

+ You have praised the miscreant for responding and allowed her/him to maintain her/his dignity.

And, of course, if the pupil still does not respond, you fall back on the 'I need' format again with the consequence carried out if s/he does not improve. So you need to be mentally agile and have that 90-second talk on the tip of your tongue, ready to employ at any given moment. It will need practice, but it is very powerful and very successful when delivered quietly, calmly and as if nothing were wrong!

You might want to time this, but here is an example an English teacher could employ. Let us assume that the lesson is about *Macbeth* (or the 'Scottish Play' if you are superstitious!) and the class has been doing some work on the witches' predictions. Gary, unfortunately, is back in your class and just will not settle to his work. You have spoken to him a couple of times, after which he has settled momentarily, then returned to his former behaviour, but each time getting a little more rowdy. You have, however, had the common sense (and you will read it in the very next section, 'The Classroom Clown') to 'isolate' Gary in one of the far corners of the classroom. The rest of the pupils in the class are working reasonably well, but Gary's behaviour is threatening to disrupt that. And please, do take this firmly on board: pupils mimic poor behaviour!

So you walk towards Gary and stop a few feet away from him. Most pupils will react to this and will give you attention for a moment. It is up to you to grasp that moment. It needs to be to the point, firmly delivered, with a consequence attached. So:

'Gary, I have already spoken to you three times this lesson. I need you to settle down, get on with your work and stop disrupting the other pupils in the class. If I have to speak to you again, I shall have to send you from the room.'

You turn away from Gary and address the rest of the class. Get your stop-watch ready as you read this out aloud:

'Right everyone look this way quickly!' (Clap your hands to draw their attention to you.) 'You should have worked out by now just what the predictions are that the witches have made to Macbeth and Banquo. You should have those written down by now. You also need to make sure that you know which of those predictions are for Macbeth and which are for Banquo. Also, you need to be aware of the way in which the predictions are beginning to affect the two men in different ways. How is Macbeth reacting to what the witches are saying and how is Banquo? What do you think this tells us about the two men?

'Macbeth is being offered something way beyond his wildest dreams: the chance to become King of Scotland. Banquo, on the other hand, is not so fortunate, because it is his sons who will be the lucky ones and not him.

'Then you need to look at what happens almost immediately after the witches have disappeared.

How to Handle Particularly Challenging Pupils

Remember, Macbeth has been greeted by the witches as the Thane of Glamis, which he is, but then as the Thane of Cawdor, which he is not. Who are the messengers who bring Macbeth and Banquo news and what do they tell Macbeth straightaway? They tell him that he is to become the new Thane of Cawdor and that the present Thane is being held for treason and is to be executed.

'Now imagine how you would feel if you were told something like what the witches had told Macbeth, and then immediately one of those things comes true. What effect does it have on Macbeth and how is it starting to fashion the way that he is thinking?'

This should be delivered in a measured, calm and matter-of-fact way. I have written this out also to allow me to point out significant moments in the monologue, which are important. One, we know that it is being delivered at this point to deal with Gary, but it is also probably a very good time to rail the rest of the class in anyway, because certainly some of them will have started to mimic Gary's behaviour, albeit in a less obvious and confrontational manner. By going for the heart of the actual content of the lesson and also mentioning, as I did in the third sentence of my delivery, that they should have already completed at least one aspect of the work in writing, you are doing two potent things: first, for those pupils who have achieved, that you are making them feel good and at ease; and second, you are sending a strong signal to the others that they are behind and need to crack on. And, of course, Gary has now had the time to settle.

At this moment in time, you might want to return to Gary and point out how little work he has accomplished thus far and offer him a helping hand, which shows that he now has the opportunity to settle down and get on, and that you do not hold a grudge against him. And, most importantly, if he still refuses to comply and continues to misbehave, you can use all of this in your explanation to him as to why you are now carrying out the sanction you warned him about earlier.

There is one additional feature I want to draw to your attention here, which I use a great deal and I believe to be one which makes youngsters think more closely about their actions. You still employ the 'I need' construction, but you add the notion of decision-making into the equation. So, instead of simply berating a pupil about her/his behaviour and attempting to bring a satisfactory resolution to the problem, you actually engage them in a simple intellectual exercise about the quality of their decision-making.

Explain to the pupil that s/he has a major advantage over any other living creature, which is the ability to make decisions. Decisions, by definition, are about making choices. We as humans can make choices; often animals are simply driven by instinct. Get the pupil (or pupils) to consider the decision-making process and how that can better influence their choices.

So, for many of the examples I have already given to you, you could quite easily add something along the lines of: 'You have made the wrong choice. I need you to think more carefully about your decision-making in future. I need you to use your ability more sensibly before you make the wrong choices again.'

You can see once again how this places a different kind of onus upon a pupil. It engages her/him on an intellectual level and it strongly suggests that you believe s/he has the mental capacity to make better decisions.

The 'Classroom Clown'

Many pupils enjoy the role of the 'classroom clown'. There are numerous reasons for this, but it is safe to say that, whatever they may be, you still have the problem of dealing with those pupils and they can be severe pains and real disruptors of lessons. You do not need to be an 'expert' or to have known the class to be able to spot the 'clown'.

The 'clown' is very often male and is usually not the most academically minded of pupils in the class. He often misbehaves to hide his own inadequacies, sometimes academically and sometimes socially, or else a combination of the two. On the social level, he thinks that behaving in this way will endear him to his peers.

Dos and Don'ts of Behaviour Management

They often see him as a fool as much as you and other teachers do.

There is a number of things to remember about this kind of character and about the urgent need to deal with him/her. In the last section I stated that pupils mimic poor behaviour. This is an absolute truism in teaching. It is the bad apple syndrome. What you have to understand is that whilst most pupils genuinely want to impress you and do want to learn, they also like a bit of 'entertainment' along the way. The 'clown' can provide that. Unfortunately, s/he does not know where to stop and before you know it your lesson can be in total disarray. That pupil is the catalyst, and in my present school will be the pupil who is most likely to be 'On-Called', which is a system we have whereby pupils can be sent to another room where there will be a teacher who will deal with all such pupils who have been sent from lessons. This system is very important, because it allows lessons to proceed without the disruptive influence of such a pupil. If the school in which you are teaching does not have such a system, then you will have to deal with the pupil yourself, and that might mean making them stand outside for a couple of minutes, re-introducing them into the room, into a different seat (see below) and spelling out firm consequences to her/him.

One of the best strategies with these characters, and I have already alluded to it several times, is to carefully plan where to place them in your classroom. I have seen many teachers put them at the front of the class, next to them. I do not agree with this strategy, because it allows these pupils to turn round and 'entertain' the class from the front. I have found a much more effective ploy is to do the exact opposite and sit these pupils at the back of the classroom in a far corner. This way they are isolated and have to look forward. If there are two such characters in your class, put them in each of the far corners with plenty of pupils in between them. You might even organize the desks or tables in the corner so that they are further apart from the other desks than usual.

The other purpose this serves is to allow the other pupils to concentrate on you, and not have this pupil between them and you, constantly causing a distraction. And of course, do not forget the 'Use of body and the 90-second' strategy, which is ideal with these pupils.

It is also very important when dealing with these characters that you speak to them before they enter the classroom. Stay calm and collected in very much the same way that I have suggested with those pupils who have been removed from your classroom for misbehaviour. Keep it brief and to the point and take them to their seats, having told them what you expect from them in terms of their behaviour and attitude.

But what happens if they do not like this new arrangement and start to object, as well they may? Think about the exit strategy (which you will read about below): don't box the pupil in. So, you might

115

decide to opt for a compromise if this is the first time, which could go like this:

> 'I was disappointed in the way you behaved last lesson and the fact that you disrupted the education of others in the class. You're telling me that you don't want to sit at the back of the class. OK! I shall let you sit where you normally sit, but the first sign of a problem and you know what will happen!'

And if that occurs, move them straight away. (If they still object, you have been given strategies for dealing with this above.)

If the pupil only mildly objects to being placed in the corner of the room, turn it round and put an educational slant on it:

> 'I am doing this to give you the best opportunity of success. You find it difficult not to get distracted where you normally sit. I want you to improve and this is the best way forward for you to be successful in this lesson.'

What you can now do, and indeed some of you might even be ahead of me, is once s/he has been put in this seat, employ the 'Use of body and the 90-second' ploy immediately. You can see that controlling pupils is a multi-layered approach and not always simply down to one particular strategy.

The Exit Strategy

If you examine the above strategy carefully, you will notice that the pupil has been given options. This is the 'Exit Strategy' and you must always use it. When dealing with a really problematic pupil, do not 'box' her/him in. What I am referring to is the habit that some teachers have of giving a pupil no way out of a situation. When a teacher does that, s/he is being unreasonable and that will be picked up by a pupil or by a whole class if this is occurring, as it often does, in full view of other pupils. You are a role model at all times, and showing youngsters the voice of reason in a calm and controlled fashion will only enhance your reputation.

Let us look at an example of how you can use the exit strategy and see if this can better describe what I need you to do if you get into this kind of situation.

The scenario is that a girl in your class is constantly misbehaving, being disruptive and basically challenging your authority. When you go through the 'I need' scenario, you need to underline to her how she can exit from this situation without losing face, and without there needing to be a consequence.

So, let's call the girl Mary:

'Mary, I have asked you politely and pleasantly to stop disrupting and to get on with your work. You are only going to make this a whole lot worse for yourself if you continue in this manner. I need you to return to your work and then I won't take any further action. I am giving you a simple choice: get on with your work sensibly or ... 'State what the consequence will be and carry it out immediately if she does not comply.

Mary has been given an 'out', an exit. You have laid that out before her slowly and carefully in a quiet, non-confrontational manner. What is more, the other pupils can see that you have been reasonable and, if you have to carry out the consequence, you can draw that to their attention. After all, this is an educational situation, from which you want them all to benefit and learn.

Let's look at Gary again, who is now misbehaving in the corridor and is reluctant to go to his next lesson:

'Gary!' (Gets his attention) 'I need you to go to your next lesson please, Gary.'

Gary may react in a whole multitude of different ways: he may go! Job done! He may claim he doesn't know where his next lesson is; he may simply refuse.

If he claims he doesn't know where his next lesson is, then say something like this:

'Gary, if that is true, I shall have to take you to [mention a senior member of staff or his Head of Year] and they can deal with you.'

Be prepared to do this. However, if he still refuses to come with you:

'Gary, this is a simple situation, which you are making a whole lot worse by behaving like this. I know you are better than this. You need to start making better decisions. I need you to come with me now and we will sort this out quietly and sensibly. If you do not come with me, you will be in a lot of trouble and there is no reason for it.'

It is now important, having delivered his 'out', not to hang around and get into a further argument. If he will not come now for you, you are only going to make it worse. Start to walk away slowly and say:

'Gary, I'm not staying any longer. You're making a really poor decision. I have told you what I want you to do, which is to come with me now and if you do so, we can sort it out. I'm going to see [mention teacher's name] now and it would be sensible if you came with me.'

Walk off slowly and do not look back. If he comes with you, do not engage in conversation with him; just take him to the member of staff and tell her/him that Gary has lost his timetable and does not know where his next lesson is. Do not try to get him into trouble or make the matter worse; he will never forgive you. If he does not come, go to that teacher and let her/him know what has happened and leave it to her/him. Next time you see Gary, acknowledge him and tell him that you were disappointed in him over that last incident and then walk off. You have kept your dignity and not lost any authority, built the bridge between you, and Gary will not feel that he has been mistreated either.

Building the Bridge

Behaviour management goes beyond dealing with a pupil or pupils. Hundreds of pupils every minute of every day are being punished in some form or other by some teacher or other in schools throughout the world. We all know this and it will always be the case. But it is this punishment that can be your undoing in terms of your ability to manage that pupil's behaviour in future. Look at it logically: by having to impose a sanction on a pupil, your relationship with her/him has momentarily fractured. It now needs to be repaired or the fracture can become more pronounced, with the result that the pupil becomes an even bigger problem.

So it is what happens after you have imposed the sanction that will determine the eventual outcome. It really does not matter how small that sanction has been, as I shall relate.

If a pupil has misbehaved during your lesson, it is important that, at or towards the end of the lesson, when everyone is packing away, you have a quiet word with that pupil and register both your disappointment with the way s/he has behaved and that you expect a better attitude next time. Spend no more than 30 seconds doing this; immediately turn away afterwards and you will prevent a potential argument or discussion on the matter. You have had the final word; the pupil has been treated with respect and has kept her/his dignity. You have rebuilt the bridge that momentarily collapsed between you.

If you have to remove a pupil from the classroom, it is of paramount importance that you speak to that pupil *before* the next lesson, because s/he could well be harbouring resentment, which will only get worse. Most schools have a system by which pupils can be sent from the classroom to another designated area in the school. When a member of staff is experiencing a particular problem with a pupil, s/he can send that pupil from the room to that other area. The problem with this system is that it dilutes the authority of the teacher who has to remove that pupil. I repeat, because it is so important: it is vital that you have a quick chat with any pupil you have had to remove from your class so that bridges can be built again between you. This must happen *before* you teach them again. The pupil will very rarely try to put the relationship right: it is up to you to do so.

Remember: keep it brief, register disappointment, talk about expectations for next lesson and state that s/he is better than the way s/he behaved. (Here is that construction again!) Do not get into a discussion.

Dos and Don'ts of Behaviour Management

Make your point, state your case, say 'Thank you' and depart. 'Thank you' is an ideal way to end a conversation. Use it, thank you!

So your chat with the pupil could go like this:

'Just a quick word, before you go into the lesson, Robert, please. I was disappointed with you last lesson. You made the wrong choices. That's behind us now. I know you are better than that. I expect a better attitude today. OK, thank you, in you go.'

It helps if you smile as well. This is short, sharp and to the point. Robert knows now that what happened in the last lesson is over and done with and there is no 'baggage' creating any problem between the two of you. Additionally, because you have been polite and pleasant and respectful, you can use all of these against him should he misbehave in the lesson that you are about to teach.

Not 'Did?' but 'Why?'

There will be times in a classroom, or when you are dealing with a situation outside of the classroom, when you are faced with a predicament where a pupil is going to challenge your authority by lying. In the classroom, this kind of situation is quite common. A pupil does something to another pupil: pokes her/him in the ribs, throws a paper ball at her/him, calls her/him a name. There will be many a time when you have seen or heard this with your own eyes or ears.

However, you will regrettably discover that many pupils will lie automatically when accused of a transgression. I have stood and witnessed a pupil kick in a glass pane in a door only for him to deny it to my face when I asked why he had done it. And here lies the key to your questioning. If you are absolutely certain that you have the right pupil, do not ask if s/he has done it; ask her/him *why* s/he did it! Think about the example I have just given of our errant pupil (oh dear, it's Gary again), and the smashed window.

If, as they often do, they lie again, say: 'I didn't ask you if you did it; I asked you why you did it!'

This statement puts the onus on the pupil whilst at the same time allowing you to stay calm, objective and able to make a much clearer judgement about the motives behind the incident. Lay upon the pupil the need for telling the truth, that the transgression is not as bad as lying, and that your relationship with her/him will be damaged if s/he continues to lie.

So, for the examples I gave above in the classroom situation, where you have actually seen or heard a pupil transgress, ask her/him: Why did you do it? S/he will almost certainly answer, 'I don't know!' Then there's your opportunity to turn this into an educational situation: get all the class to listen to you and stress the importance of thinking before we act, thinking before we speak, making better decisions affecting our choice of actions and, of course, telling the truth.

It does not always work, but I guarantee it will be more likely to be successful and it will also get pupils thinking a little more carefully about lying in future, as well as simply thinking more carefully about repeating their actions.

Build upon Success rather than Dwelling on Failure

Pupils who misbehave know they do! They do not need constant reminders of this. However, that is precisely what we tend to give them. Not only that, but we all too frequently drag up their past misdemeanours and throw these at them at every opportunity.

What is far more productive is to build upon the times when pupils are actually successful, and get them to examine how this has occurred and to attempt to create a more upbeat and positive attitude towards themselves. And (as I have already mentioned in an earlier section of this book) if you label a pupil, s/he will become that label.

One of the ways that I achieve this positive change is to make pupils think about their own learning and how they can raise their levels of achievement. This immediately prevents these meetings being opportunities for simply parading their faults in front of them, and allows the pupils to focus on ways forward.

How to Handle Particularly Challenging Pupils

Even the worst behaved pupils will have those teachers and those lessons where they are successful, where they actually achieve, where they learn. It is on these that you need to concentrate with them. The person who can do this most effectively is the form tutor. In a secondary school, the form tutor, in my opinion, is the single most important role in the school. Good, conscientious form tutors can make the difference, because they care, they make time for their tutees and they have the ability to offer constructive advice: and this kind of meeting is one essential way in which they can do this. (I have dedicated a chapter to the role of the form tutor later on.)

A typical scenario is a pupil who is a well-known low-level disruptor being sent to you, or that pupil is in your tutor group and you need to talk to her/him. What normally occurs here is that the form tutor will go over what the latest incident has been, and even recount previous misdemeanours for good measure. As I have stated, this pupil knows s/he is a problem; heaven only knows how many times s/he may be reminded of that in a day, week, term, year. However, you could gloss over the 'bad bits' pretty quickly and the conversation could go something like this:

'So Susan, I see you were put out of Mrs Smith's lesson yesterday for disruption and then defiance.' (These are the two main types of pupil misbehaviour in classes.) 'That was one lesson, Susan. That means there were four other lessons where you were not removed from the classroom. How come you managed

125

to behave well enough not to be a big enough problem that you had to be removed from those lessons?'

You then need to tease out answers to this and other similar questions. What you are trying to do is to show the pupil that they actually behave more than they misbehave and what needs to be done is to build upon those positive experiences, and make them more frequent. This gives the pupil a chance, a window of opportunity. The pupil no longer feels that s/he is a total disaster; in fact s/he can see that s/he is not. The next trick is to try and get her/him to realize and understand why s/he behaves in certain ways at certain times. This goes back to the decision-making and making better choices scenario. Then build upon this and try and get her/him to recognize the signals that normally determine that the wheels are about to come off for her/him in that particular situation, and discuss what to do then.

In this way you are giving the pupil ways and means to improve rather than simply telling her/him that s/he is naughty and s/he must improve. It doesn't work like that!

The Calm Culture versus the Shouting Culture

There will be times when you have to raise your voice. With me, it's usually when I am in the yard and I need to be heard over a large expanse. If you have to raise your voice with a pupil, you must stay in control yourself in that situation, and seconds later return to talking calmly, quietly and respectfully. Remember to build the bridge with this pupil afterwards. No-one likes being shouted at and it can leave a lasting detrimental impact.

Basically shouting is a big no-no! It really does not work and you need to accept this from an early stage. When I wander around the school, it is the teachers I can hear who are having the problems. Noise generates noise! As a rule of thumb, the quieter you are, the quieter they are. It's all part of establishing a peaceful, productive atmosphere, where calm is the aim. This is the ideal working environment and you must endeavour to inculcate this in your pupils all the time. When it is like this, praise them as a class for it! Never stop aiming for this environment and always praise when it is achieved.

The major problem when you shout is that you as the adult are displaying poor communication skills and setting a poor example. The other problem is that most people have lost control when they shout, and often shouting can be equated with anger and frustration. I hear it a lot from staff who are finding it difficult to control the class. Believe me; shouting at pupils will not help. In fact, it will make matters worse. They will see that you have lost control and they will feed on it. And remember: if you're shouting and screaming at a pupil, you are the last person who should be dealing with the pupil at that time!

Keep your Head! Stay Calm when Dealing with the 'Bad' Class

You find yourself in front of the 'class from hell'! It seems that they are all misbehaving and the scene takes on riot proportions in your head. You can feel your emotions getting the better of you. Do not give into them! This is your amygdala getting the upper hand.

The amygdala is that part of your brain which deals with emotions. It is a primeval element within our psyche. The amygdala emits signals to the body and to the mind: our heartbeat increases; our muscles tense up; there is sometimes a desire to flee from the situation. So when the amygdala is activated, it has the effect of rendering you intellectually impaired. Response to a sexual situation triggers an amygdala response, which is why so many 'important' people end up in trouble: Bill Clinton is a classic example. President of the United States of America and fooling around in the White House with an aide! Pure amygdala! Do I need to say more?

When you are confronted by a class, or even one pupil, you need to be aware of whether that class or that pupil is eliciting an amygdala response within you. If it does, you are in trouble. Not just because of that single situation, but because that situation with this pupil or this class can become what is termed a 'learned response'. In other words, just the thought of teaching that pupil or class can begin to create this emotional state within you, which is precisely not the state to be in before you actually present yourself in the teaching situation. If you find yourself feeling like this before you teach a group, you need to mentally switch off, take deep breaths and try and clear your mind.

You have to maintain self-control and try and stay outwardly calm. I say 'outwardly calm', because inside you are like a bubbling cauldron. Take some deep breaths – and I mean that literally – stay calm and speak evenly. Do not outwardly panic or show that you are flustered. The calmer you appear the better the chance of achieving some semblance of order. You must trust me on this one: lose control and start to scream and shout and you are gone! It will not be easy, but staying calm is the key. It might be relevant here to draw your attention to the next section, 'When All Else Fails'. You will read about my very real experiences and see how I managed to control the amygdala and come out of those situations relatively unscathed, especially the one with the abusive girl. The only thing that saved me was the fact that I outwardly remained calm.

If some of the class have settled, thank them for that and turn your attention towards the pupil who you believe to be the main problem. Always try and bring it down to one or two at most. Use the 'I need' approach, give the pupil or pupils the consequence if they will not comply and then carry it out. The consequence could well be removal from the room, either for a couple of minutes or permanently. But whatever it is, do it calmly and coolly. Then return to the rest of the class as if nothing had happened. They will have assessed how you have managed the situation and they will be impressed that you did not lose your temper or control.

If you have temporarily removed a pupil from the room (never for more than a few minutes), go outside, speak to her/him quietly, use 'I need' again and return her/him into the room into a far corner. At the end of the lesson, have a very quick and quiet word with her/him explaining that you expect better from them the next time. If the pupil has been removed from the whole lesson, then you need to speak to her/him *before* the next lesson and establish expectations with her/him. Sometimes this is better in the presence of a Head of Year or senior member of staff to ensure that the pupil listens.

If you have managed to stay calm, cool and collected through this experience, you either already are or will be an excellent teacher and you have already taken some gigantic strides towards achieving that.

However, there can be situations where it is not just one or two pupils; you genuinely do have a 'bad class'. It is worth mentioning here that these groups of children are often self-inflicted, and by that I mean that the school's streaming, tiering or grouping systems create bonded groups of poorly motivated, disruptive and generally non-academic pupils. What is even worse, and unforgivable in my opinion, is that there are often quite able pupils in these groups, who have been put there because of their attitude and poor behaviour. What a mix! These groups tend to be together for the majority of the timetable throughout their five years in a secondary school. They learn poor behaviour from each other. They know that they have been educationally discarded. Pupils are not fools and I am always amazed that we sometimes treat them as such. These pupils are all too aware that they are the no-hopers, that they often get what they consider to be the 'poorer' teachers, that their results are the worst in the school. And what does this breed? Apathy, a 'don't give a damn' attitude, no hope, unruly behaviour and a teaching group that only very few staff in the school can manage. And you might very well be in charge of such a group. So what do you do?

The first thing to do is to be pragmatic and sensitive to the needs of these pupils. It will almost certainly be the case that many of these youngsters will have weak literacy and numeracy skills and, consequently, will not achieve much in external examinations. It is imperative that you talk with your Head of Department and determine what kind of curriculum you are going to follow. These pupils do not want to be patronized but, on the other hand, it is pointless banging on with an academic syllabus way above their heads. So the curriculum needs to be pitched just right, with a major accent on literacy and numeracy. The next thing, and this should be abundantly obvious to you by now, is that these lessons need to be the most well-planned and prepared ones of your week! There is no room for complacency with these groups. Go in under-prepared and with no back-up, and you will be sunk without a trace. Make sure that your lessons really are a series of small chunks and teach them as such. These lessons need to be interesting, pacy, punchy, and above all, fun!

It may not come as a surprise to you, but I have taught groups like this all my teaching career, because it was felt that I could control them. This is a misnomer; if I have been successful with these groups, it is because I have been able to motivate them, bring them on board and make them feel valued. What I have always done on the first encounter in that first lesson with them is to challenge them. There is no point trying to disguise what group they are in or why they are there. As I said: they know all too well! What I do is to turn that round: 'Are you happy being in this group? You shouldn't be! I'm going to challenge each and every one of you! I'm going to challenge you to show everyone in this school that you are better than being in this group suggests. And we are going to do this together.'

It is amazing the effect it has on them. And you have to keep on with this approach every lesson. The pupils no longer feel disenfranchized. They now feel a little special. They feel that someone actually cares. It is a transformational moment for them, because too many of their teachers add to their feelings of inadequacy, rather than inspiring them to do better.

To be anecdotal again, I had a rather strange experience a couple of years ago, when the then Head of English decided, without any discussion, to create a 'dump group' (for want of a better expression) of all the really disaffected boys in Year 9. And guess which teacher was given that group? Well done! He simply came up to me on this particular Wednesday morning, handed me a class list with these boys' names on it and told me that this would commence Period 5 that afternoon. The other thing to mention is that I was to have them for four one-hour lessons a week!

Believe me, you could not have contrived a more challenging group of pupils! I can remember quite clearly that first lesson. The boys sloped into the room, looked at each other in dumb amazement and then at me. They knew the score. They knew that they had been cast adrift and that the head of the school's pastoral system had been chosen to keep them under control, thus allowing the other classes not to be disrupted. And they were spot on! I delivered an inspirational speech to them of Churchillian proportions. I told them precisely why they were there and told them that they had to prove people wrong. What was even worse, because our educational lords and masters believe that youngsters need a diet of Shakespeare, I had to start their KS3 SATs work with, yes you've guessed it, *Macbeth*! Thank goodness the DCSF has recently come to its collective senses and scrapped KS3 SATS!

There was not a lesson when I did not exhort them to higher and better things and, astonishingly, over two-thirds of them achieved a Level 4 in their English, and two of them were only a fraction away from Level 5. It may not appear to be that mind-boggling, but believe me, I regard it as one of my finest educational hours!

Dos and Don'ts of Behaviour Management

So what am I saying here? This is a situation where you desperately need to be pro-active. Your lessons really do need to be interesting and engaging; you cannot rely on these pupils providing the spark. You have to make them feel important and wanted, as opposed to cast off and hung out to dry. Try and be a little more relaxed with them also. Be prepared to give these groups a 'reward' at the end of each lesson. The last ten minutes of each of my lessons was 'reward' time for effort, attitude and hard work. We would have 'swapping experiences time' and believe me, not only was that interesting, it was incredibly eye-opening too. I don't see the educational advantage to word searches, but I would not object to them as a last-ten-minute reward. You might give them a quick quiz or let them do some puzzles. However, make sure that they have earned the reward. Do not give it otherwise, because you will only inculcate bad habits.

And when pupils do not behave, you always have the disappointment card to play: and with groups like these, it can be devastatingly effective, because you have shown them that you care, that you have their interests at heart. They will know this and you may well be one of very few of their teachers whom they believe to be like this. You can use the disappointment card with them as a whole group much more than as individuals, because you are using the very thing that has created the problem in the first place, the bonded group, to your advantage.

When All Else Fails!

So, you've followed all the advice I have given to you, but you are still having major problems with a particular pupil, group of pupils or class. The first thing to instil into your own conscience is that you are not the only teacher in the school who is experiencing this. Sadly, many teachers actually do think this! Second, if you are new either to the profession or to that school, and also depending on the kind of school in which you are trying to teach, there will be a period of time for adjustment and learning. I have taught in four schools and each time I moved, I had to adjust to my new school, start afresh with pupils I had never met and who had never encountered me, become accustomed to the systems in the school, become familiar with the lay-out of the school and also try and engage with my fellow teachers. This is no different to any job.

In my experience, the first half term is the most stressful and demanding for all the reasons I have just given, but mainly because the pupils are testing you: trying you out, seeing what you are worth. I mentioned skirmishing in an earlier chapter and these first few weeks are very much akin to that. Generally, if you follow my advice, you will find that the pupils will have largely accepted you by the time you are into your second half term. It incrementally improves throughout your first year, half term by half term, and then you come back into your second year and it is

135

exponentially better. You are now very much one of the school in the pupils' eyes. I tell every newly qualified teacher that and not one of them has ever found it to be different. The collective experience of scores of teachers must stand for something. The other thing I impress upon them is that they must be genuine with pupils, take an interest in them and be consistent. Of course, I also give them as much of the advice contained in this book as I can.

However, let's consider the possibility that you are in your second year and you are still experiencing the kind of difficulty with which I started this chapter. What do you do now? Let me get anecdotal for a while. I am doing this so that you know that all teachers experience difficulties at some time or another, irrespective of experience, confidence or levels of pupil management. Here are some of mine, lest you believe me to be someone who has been immune from such devastating encounters and to be a paradigm of pedagogical perfection! I shall relate what I did about it and how I learnt from the situations.

My final teaching practice in 1972 saw me at a large, 3000-strong comprehensive in the North East of England. My first two teaching practices had been in a primary and then a middle school, and had gone really well. I thought I was the best teacher since the advent of education. How things were to be rudely interrupted!

It was a six-week practice and I was going to teach Drama and P.E.. This could not have represented a greater contrast, because the Head of P.E. was superb (recall that I mentioned his influence on me) and the Head of Drama, though an extremely pleasant man, was a disaster when it came to organization and pupil control. So I went from the educationally sublime to the educationally ridiculous: when I taught P.E., I was in control and the lessons were wonderful to be involved in. However, when I taught Drama, it was a living nightmare. The pupils were already in the drama studio, climbing all over the place, screaming, fighting: it was like walking into a children's play den. It was virtually impossible to even get the pupils to hear you. On top of that I had three Year 8 classes to teach in Drama and, incredibly, these three classes were on the staffroom noticeboard as classes not to be given to students or supply staff if at all possible. I should add that they were not the only classes mentioned in this way!

All lessons were one hour in duration. How long is an hour? Ask a teacher with any class like I am mentioning! My first encounter with one of these classes was so unbelievably bad that I nearly packed it in there and then. I spent the whole hour going from one group to another, trying to get them to be quiet and sit down. All to no avail. I left the room and sought the Head of Department. He wasn't around. The location of the drama studio made it virtually impossible to leave and find another teacher. Besides, I was so concerned that I would fail my teaching practice if anyone actually saw this mess that I decided not to go further afield for assistance, which would involve leaving the pupils to themselves.

I went to see the Head of P.E. and sought his advice. If you can't be heard, blow a whistle. OK. See the Head of Drama (he did it for me) and ensure that first, the door to the studio was locked thus denying pupils access, and second, I had a key. This happened. Get to the studio before the pupils arrived. Speak to them before they go into the studio. Forget about teaching them Drama for a while, talk to them, develop a relationship, tell them a bit about yourself, engage them in interesting conversation. And believe it or not, it worked. It was a close-run thing, because my tutor from college could have popped in at any time. Fortunately he saw me teach P.E. in my first two weeks and Drama in two of the last four, and by that time the pupils were greatly improved.

My first teaching appointment was in January 1973. It was also in the North East, and in a school regarded as one of the toughest in the country. After I had left (and I hasten to add, this had nothing to do with my departure!) it was closed. It also featured in a television documentary and was subsequently re-opened with a new name, new head, and new railings around its perimeter, probably to keep the pupils in as much as unwanted elements out. It has been closed again since then!

I was appointed as a P.E. teacher, simply because I was physically the biggest there in the interview, and I had 'proven' myself at that other school on my final teaching practice. P.E. was not my main subject, but that did not come into the equation. As I said, I was the biggest of the applicants!

In my first week, three boys tried to assault me individually on three separate occasions. I can remember their names to this day, and the exact days and times as well. I had not provoked the situation. I had not even met any of these three before they arrived at the gym and 'went' for me. I won't go into details, save to say that I fronted up to them, stood tall and firm and did not give an inch. My new career depended on the outcome of these encounters. There is no doubt that nowadays all three of these pupils would be permanently excluded. I didn't even report them! The outcome was that word got round the school that you didn't mess with the new P.E. teacher, and I went on to experience three great years there.

But there were three staff there, my Head of Department, and two Georges, who became my mentors. I bled them dry for advice, support and ultimately friendship. So the lesson is here: if you can deal with a problem yourself, you will be seen as someone who is in charge; whenever you pass a pupil on to someone else, you always dilute your authority somewhat. And no, that does not mean you don't pass a pupil on, but you must stamp your authority first before you do so. And always seek advice, help and support.

My final experience was probably the most shocking of all, because it was in my first week as a senior teacher in my previous school and I was appointed to improve pupil behaviour! Imagine then how I felt when this Year 10 girl, on being asked to 'Sit down over here, please', regaled me with a torrent of verbal abuse at a level I had hitherto never encountered. She point-blank refused to do anything, trashed a printer, flung books around the room and continued her tirade of abuse at me. So what do you do in such a position? The answer is multi-layered. First, you must recognize that this is not a personal attack upon you as the teacher. Now I know that is difficult – believe me, I know! But it is the truth. This pupil is emotionally supercharged and you are the unfortunate person who is going to have to take the outburst. Second, do not inflame the situation by becoming aggressive, authoritarian or confrontational. Send a pupil to get another member of staff. Talk quietly and respectfully to the pupil throughout. Try and calm her/him down. Find out what the pupil's name is from another pupil if you don't know it. Use the pupil's name every time you speak to her/him. When the other teacher arrives, ask her/him to take the rest of the pupils out of the room, or, if that teacher has a good or better relationship with the pupil in question, you take the pupils out of the room and allow the other teacher to take over. As it turned out the then Head of Year 8 arrived on the scene and, because of his relationship with the vast majority of the pupils in the school and the respect they had (and still have) for him, the girl went quietly off with him. I felt shell-shocked. How could I possibly continue?

How to Handle Particularly Challenging Pupils

Well I could and I did. You see, despite the horrendous nature of the incident and the fact that the girl at no time listened to me, respected my authority or in any way tempered her behaviour or language, I never lost my personal control (at least externally; inside was a turmoil!), and never lost my self-respect or dignity in the eyes of the other pupils, nor indeed in the girl's eyes when I next saw her and spoke to her about the incident. Incredibly, she was always well-behaved for me after that. I say 'incredibly', but it isn't, because of the way I had reacted. When she calmed down, she was ashamed of the way she had behaved and, because I had remained outwardly calm and had never once raised my voice in anger at her, she found it far easier to accept me. Additionally, and one thing that I really had to do to maintain any credibility in the eyes of the rest of the class, I had to bring them back in like nothing had happened and get on with the lesson. That wasn't easy, as this was a two-hour all-afternoon lesson and there were still some ninety minutes left. But I managed it and there was no carry-over into the way other pupils perceived me. By that I mean that I had not lost any of my authority or standing in the school community, and this was because I had managed the situation calmly. If I had lost control, screamed or shouted and shown signs of being totally flustered by what had occurred, that would have been the very weakness the rest of that class would have recognized and ultimately exploited.

Dos and Don'ts of Behaviour Management

So, what can you learn from this?

+ Stay calm.

+ Keep your self-respect and dignity.

+ Speak quietly to the pupil.

+ Use the pupil's name.

+ Try and calm the pupil down.

+ Give the pupil space – do *not* get close to her/him.

+ Send a pupil to find another teacher.

+ Either you or that teacher take the rest of the class out of the room or area – the last thing you need is an audience.

+ A senior teacher should be informed as soon as possible.

+ Go back in with the rest of the class when the situation has been resolved.

+ Try your very hardest to continue with the lesson – I know this is difficult.

+ You may have to calm the other pupils down as well, because the incident will have also shocked some of them.

+ Speak to the pupil who had the outburst at some later stage to talk through the incident.

- This will build the bridge between you and that pupil and it will show her/him that you harbour no resentment.

- It will also show that you respect the pupil and s/he will register that subliminally.

- Do talk to a senior member of staff whom you trust and respect, because you will need a sympathetic ear and an encouraging word after such an event.

I personally learnt a great deal from this predicament. I have also had to go into classes since then and deal with pupils who are behaving in the same manner. I stress, because it is of paramount importance, that this is not a personal attack on you! The pupil is venting her/his spleen because of a wide variety of external issues and factors. You just happen to be in the firing line. But it does raise an equally crucial skill, which is 'reading the signs'.

Reading the Signs

I mentioned earlier the need for being aware of GAT and SEN pupils in your classes. The SEN register is not just there for legal purposes; it is a vital information pack. Get to know your SENCO and have a word with her/him. You can go through your class lists and highlight the SEN pupils and what their particular special need is. Most of them will be for some learning difficulty; others will be for general misbehaviour, and some will be for emotional difficulties. You might like to ask your SENCO how these 'difficulties' might manifest themselves in a classroom situation and what triggers them off. This is important information, which few teachers take time to arm themselves with. I personally know every one of these pupils in my school, how they can behave and also what generally triggers the situation. It would help if their classroom teachers did as well; it might prevent some of the confrontations occurring in the first place.

Let us suppose that you have done all that. A classroom is a busy environment and there is a plethora of potential scenarios that can be played at any one time. Please, try and be a teacher who is observant. I have already stated that you should try and meet and greet pupils when they come to your lesson. How does each individual respond to you? Are there any tell-tale signs here? Body language is a sure displayer of how somebody is feeling. Observe that in your pupils, especially those who you know have a 'history'. Look where your pupils decide to sit in the room. If you have not put them into designated seats, how do they choose to seat themselves? Has one pupil decided to sit apart from everyone else? Is this usual? Are some of them still wearing their outdoor coats or wearing a cap?

Now be very careful! It is one thing being tuned in and aware that there is a potential problem about to ensue, it is another how you handle it! Knowing there is the likelihood of a particular pupil having an outburst does give you an advantage, but only if you tread warily and carefully. It is not too dramatic for me to ask you to see this pupil as a time bomb, which can literally explode at any moment. You need to organize around that pupil. You need to manage the other pupils to prevent any one of them being the catalyst. And you need to manage yourself. You do not want to say the wrong thing at precisely the wrong time. You will have to learn from experience when it is best to leave it alone and say nothing, and when it is best to offer a sympathetic voice and an exit strategy. If it is the latter, the exit strategy would be for that particular pupil to leave the room and go somewhere else, not as a punishment, but as a quiet place to be able to have some time to her/himself. If you do this, you must inform a senior teacher, preferably the SENCO or the pupil's Head of Year. We do not want a pupil like this going off by her/himself. You might have to send a responsible pupil to go and fetch another member of staff to facilitate this. If you do send another pupil, ask them very quietly to carry out your errand. Do it otherwise and you can inflame the situation immediately.

I am sure that you can see this is a better situation than having no idea about the pupil, not reading the signs and suddenly having to face an emotional outburst that takes the wind completely out of your sails. And, even if you have done all that I have advised, this will still happen, because there is nothing more unpredictable than people. But at least you now know how to deal with this kind of situation.

145

6 Behaviour Management at a Glance

General Strategies at a Glance

- Make sure pupils have a clear understanding of your expectations; expectations are more potent than rules.

- Your three most important words are 'Please' and 'Thank you'.

- Remember: be firm *but* fair.

- Do not strip away a pupil's dignity; s/he will not forgive you.

- Always try and give pupils an exit route; do not corner them and allow no escape from their situation.

- Always have a reason why you are doing anything; pupils ask, and to reply with 'Because I said so' is not a viable response.

- Avoid confrontations, especially those you may not win!

- Remember, if you feel you've lost control, the pupils will know this.

- Always try and keep calm, quiet and dignified, especially when the going gets tough.

- If you shout and/or scream at a pupil, you are more likely to get a similar reaction in return – and you stand more chance of losing general control as well.

- Pupils who are late should be made to sign a late sheet, and at the end of the lesson tell them that they will be reported to their Head of Year, or what punishment you are going to hand out (e.g. a break-time detention).

- Prepare a seating plan for each of your 'problem' classes – the real troublemakers are sometimes best seated in the far corners of a classroom, where they cannot turn round and disrupt and they have to look forward.

- Be prepared to stand quietly and wait for the pupils to settle on occasion – remember your noise can increase theirs!

- Do not invade pupils' space when they are misbehaving; keep your distance from them – no closer than an arm's length away.

Dos and Don'ts of Behaviour Management

◆ Speak quietly but firmly to them, using the first person 'I' and not the second person 'you'. So: 'I need you to get on with your work' is much more potent than 'Will you get on with your work?' The second is likely to receive a response in the negative: 'No!' The first 'I need' is a psychologically more powerful statement that puts you in control, not the pupil. The use of 'thank you' at the end of your instruction signals a closure to the conversation.

◆ Do not isolate pupils in your classroom by having them stand in corners: it will backfire and is more likely to be unsuccessful as it only draws attention to them, which is probably what they want anyway.

◆ Make eye contact with each pupil in your classroom when talking to them every 40 seconds or so; the second they are not looking at you or are distracted, ask them a question, make them stand up and then tell them why you have made them do that.

◆ If a pupil is still misbehaving, turn whatever they are doing into 'an instruction': 'I need you to stop disturbing others and I need you to get on quietly with your work, thank you!' This should be said about an arm's length from the pupil, quietly and firmly staring directly at her/him. Immediately move away by turning your body and address the rest of the class for between 60–90 seconds. This will give the miscreant time to settle down.

◆ A 30-second chat with the pupil at the end of the lesson and/or at the start of the next is always necessary where you feel that s/he has not met your expectations.

◆ Tell pupils that they are better than the way they are behaving.

◆ If you have to remove a pupil from your classroom or have her/him removed by another member of staff, have a word with that pupil as s/he enters your classroom next time: 'I was disappointed with your behaviour last lesson. That's behind us. I need us to move on today!' or words to that effect.

◆ Do not detain pupils at the end of the morning session or at the end of the day – it is illegal to do so if you have not contacted home. Pupils can be detained on the same day, provided home has been contacted and permission granted.

◆ If you remove a pupil from your room, it should be for a maximum of two to three minutes. This is not a sanction that should extend beyond that time. Do not send a pupil out for an indefinite period of time unless s/he is being removed to another area of the school with another member of staff.

◆ Make sure you are thoroughly familiar with all the school's disciplinary systems.

Possible Actions and Sanctions to Use

I have referred to the use of sanctions and actions you can take throughout the book, and have mentioned some along the way. I thought it might be useful to list the different kinds of sanctions you could employ, and the occasions and misdemeanours for which I believe they would be appropriate.

- *Stand quietly and stare at pupil.* Ideal for minor indiscretions; very powerful when you have good control over a class normally.

- *Quiet word with a pupil.* Use for first misdemeanours; allows pupil to maintain dignity.

- *Walk up to pupil and deliver warning.* For a persistent disruptor; consider use of body and 90-second rule as well.

- *Isolate pupil in the classroom.* For a persistent disruptor; actually separate the pupil from others; do not make them stand in a corner; sends signal to rest of class that you are doing something.

- *Send pupil out of room.* For a persistent disruptor; you need to remove pupil from room to avoid her/his behaviour acting as a catalyst; do not send pupils out for longer than a couple of minutes.

- *Removal from room to another teacher or area in school.* For a persistent disruptor, or verbal abuse to you or another pupil, or a pupil refusing to do work.

- *Break-time detention.* An excellent sanction, because it does not need anyone's permission to do it and is a massive inconvenience to the pupil; also make sure the rest of the class knows that it has occurred.

- *After-school detention.* This is fraught with potential problems; you need to let the parent/carer know; however, it can be carried out that same day, provided the parent/carer gives permission.

- *Referral to Head of Department.* Useful if you have a strong Head of Department and you can be there at the time the pupil is spoken to.

- *Referral to Head of Year.* As above.

- *Referral to Senior Management.* Only in extreme cases, usually involving verbal abuse, some kind of assault or gross misbehaviour.

But please, please: do not give them lines! It is meaningless, it is pointless and, as an English teacher, I wouldn't thank you for using my subject as a means of punishment!

Avoiding Confrontation

I am sure you will be familiar with this situation, whether it occurs in the teaching arena or at home with your own children. What should be a very brief and concise demonstration of disapproval, turns into a fully

Dos and Don'ts of Behaviour Management

fledged argument leaving both parties upset, disgruntled and parting on unresolved terms. In the teaching situation, this is something which happens far too often and the corollary is never to anyone's advantage; it tends to lead to a disintegration of relationships, which are the cornerstone of all good behaviour management strategies.

Let me give you the scenario. A pupil is not behaving as the teacher expects. The teacher decides to remove the pupil from the classroom for a minute in order to make a point. The teacher then goes out onto the corridor to 'talk' to the pupil. Now I say 'talk', because herein lies the problem. First, we need to sort out a few simple, home truths. This is a problem pupil, at least for you and at least on this particular day, in this particular lesson. There may be a host of mitigating circumstances and reasons why this is the case but, quite honestly, you do not have the time, and this certainly is not the place to be considering them. Your task is to ensure that the pupil is going to come back into your room in a more settled frame of mind. The pupil has had a minute to settle down outside. You have chosen this action because it takes away the pupil's audience, gives the pupil a chance to calm down and gives you the chance to collect your own thoughts. All of this is good practice and you have not left the pupil outside the room for too long (a big mistake, because youngsters get bored and resentful out on the corridor and can interrupt other lessons, just walk off or give you a hard time when you come out to speak to them).

So, out you come and you start your 'talk'. Unfortunately, and I am absolutely positive that you have witnessed or experienced this: the pupil starts to put her/his side of the events. The teacher feels the need to defend her/his action of removing the pupil from the room and enters into an onslaught about the pupil's behaviour, attitude, inability to work with others – the list is pretty exhaustive. The pupil is having none of this and stands her/his ground.

Before a minute has passed, we have an argument on our hands, which can soon develop into a heated exchange. Now, who is the winner in this situation? No one. Certainly not you, the teacher. The pupil will resent you and your relationship with the pupil will be damaged; the chances are another teacher will have to deal with the pupil. None of this is beneficial and yet there are staff, regrettably, who adopt this approach almost as standard practice. Don't I know it? Because I am the member of staff who generally has to pick up the pieces, and I can tell you that the pupils I pick up from these situations really, really dislike the teacher responsible for this. These pupils become very blin-kered at these times and adopt a very human stance of blaming everyone else but themselves. My job then is to try and superglue the relationship between the teacher and pupil, and we all know that anything once broken does not repair like new.

So what should I do in this situation, I hear you cry? The answer is so simple and should become a natural part of your armoury and you should use it in a plethora of different situations, as I will shortly outline. What you do is to keep this 'talk' extremely brief and do not give the pupil any chance whatsoever of responding. You do not do this in a rude or overly officious manner; you do not talk down to the pupil or strip away her/his dignity. This is a very quiet but firm 10 to 15 second talking to and it is delivered very quietly.

Here is how it should go, and the pupil who has been standing outside your room for a minute is Robert:

'Robert, I'm very disappointed in your attitude this lesson. You're better than that. Follow me in, go to your seat and let's see what you are really capable of.'

THE END!

You then turn immediately away from Robert, not giving him any chance of responding to what you have said. Even if he does start to speak, you have turned away and you are not going to turn back under any circumstance whatsoever. You walk into the room in front of him (and I sincerely hope that you will have remembered what to do next – the 90-second rule, Chapter 5) which is to address the whole of the class about the work in which they are engaged, which in turn will allow Robert to settle down in his place. Do not let Robert go into the room in front of you, because this allows him to be the focus of attention and all too often that will play straight back into the pupil's hands, giving the pupil the opportunity to be the clown or the centre of attention, which is often the reason why these pupils are a problem in lessons in the first place. By going into the room before Robert, you are projecting your superiority in this situation to all the pupils in the class, both on a very visible level and in a subliminal way. It demonstrates that you are in control of the situation; you are not phased by it; you have handled it calmly and collectedly. Job done!

By doing it in this way, you have also made your point to Robert: you have treated him respectfully; you have told him you value him and you have told him he has another chance. More often than not, the pupil will accept this. Of course, if a pupil does not, then you are going to have to issue a warning and carry out a sanction if the behaviour continues.

I am sure you can see the value in this approach and the potential minefield of the other way of handling these situations. What we are doing is minimizing the risk of what should be a routine talking-to turning into a major, ugly confrontation. A frequently used military expression sums this up: minimizing the collateral damage. After I had done this demonstration with staff on a training session on behaviour management, a colleague of mine suggested that we should get some bouncers from the local nightclubs to come into school and do a session with the staff on how to avoid confrontation. His spin on this was that these people have to adopt ways to take the heat out of situations, rather than adding fuel to the flames. Sadly, the bouncers were too shy to accept the invitation! It would have been interesting if they had accepted, and, I am sure, very valuable as well; these skills are transferable and are not just skills we employ in teaching.

We can employ this tactic in different situations in the school context. Obviously, the first one that springs to mind is in the classroom itself. Naturally, in the classroom situation it is potentially far worse than you ending up in an argument outside of your room with a pupil, because it is occurring in full view of an audience: the rest of the class. Youngsters are very adept at coming up with strategies that will deflect from the business at hand, which usually having to get on with the work that has been set by you. And let us be absolutely clear here: it is when you want the pupils to work that there is likely to be the greatest tension and possibility for disruption. Look again at Chapter 3 on what constitutes a good lesson to ease that tension, but for here and now what we want to avoid is a face-to-face confrontation in the classroom.

So we need to use the same tactic in the classroom as outside on the corridor. A brief 10 seconds to register your expectations and your disappointment; then physically move away from the pupil and address the whole class immediately afterwards. I have told you how to use this strategy before (see Chapter 5, The Use of Your Body and the 90-Second Rule) but, when coupled with this approach, it maximizes its effectiveness; it keeps you in control; it reduces the risk of unwanted confrontation; it reduces the risk of the situation spiralling out of control.

You can also employ this strategy on the corridor when you come across a pupil or pupils misbehaving in some way. Have your say, make your point and then move away from the situation. This is an ideal way of dealing with low-level problems that frequently occur on a corridor, and especially for those staff who do not have what the pupils would see as 'real' authority. In my school we have student supervisors who are not teachers, but whose task is to assist in the management of pupils on corridors between lessons. This is not an easy task for them, because the pupils do not see them as having any real authority whatsoever.

However, these supervisors do an incredibly good job. I have done behaviour management training with them and all, bar one of them, has adopted whole-heartedly what I have suggested to them in that training. I think you can guess what I am about to say! Everyone one of them, bar that one, has developed excellent working relationships with the youngsters and manage them with respect, dignity and good grace and, in return, receive a willingness to cooperate from the student body that is as remarkable as it is necessary. Sadly, the odd one out does not enjoy the same success, because that person is confrontational, aggressive in manner and the pupils reply in kind. If ever I needed a clear example of how to deal and how not to deal with youngsters, it is encapsulated in these people and their different approaches.

Dos and Don'ts of Behaviour Management

To summarize: confrontation rarely works. Even if you are a clearly recognizable authority figure in the school, being confrontational with youngsters may work for you at that given moment in time, but it will certainly store up problems for your colleagues.

7   The Management of Other Situations

Teaching is a complete package; it is not any one thing, but rather a whole collection of parts that go to make the whole. The remainder of this book deals with other situations that you will in some cases definitely encounter; others I hope you never do. However, if you are unfortunate enough to be confronted with a fight or an assault, whether it is on another pupil or, heaven forbid, a member of staff, I trust the advice I give you will be invaluable. Forewarned is forearmed!

The other thing to register is that every single time you are in the company of youngsters you are involved in managing them. Your consistency of approach, calmness and confidence in dealing with whatever fate throws your way will all go to produce this person, this teacher, in whom your charges will develop that trust and respect and the feeling of security which you will engender.

The Role of the Form Tutor

Most schools, but not all, commence each morning and afternoon session with a registration time when a teacher has responsibility for a group of youngsters in her/his charge. I believe the role of the form tutor to be the single most important influence on a school's ethos and on the overall behaviour, attitude and responsible nature of the student body. No single teacher has a greater effect and impact than this person. It is not exaggerating at all to say that a group of pupils with a dedicated form tutor, or classroom teacher in the primary sector, can be given a huge and significant advantage and boost over those pupils who are not as fortunate.

All of the advice I have given in this book is as germane to the form tutor in the classroom as anywhere else. You have a pivotal role to perform and how you discharge it can affect the way those pupils behave, not only with you, but also with other teachers and adults.

There is every chance in the secondary sector that you will be a form tutor. In the primary sector you will be that and their class teacher too. As I have just mentioned, this role is a crucial one. You, as a form tutor, have the chance to gain trust, respect and develop relationships that can be as rewarding to you as they are beneficial to your tutees and other staff too.

You will normally be the first person with whom they come into contact at the start of most morning and afternoon sessions. As such, it is vitally important that the six Ps (Perfect Planning and Preparation Prevents Poor Performance) are very much a part of you in that role. You will normally have 10 or 15 minutes to maximize your impact upon your charges. Use this time well; here is a checklist of some of the things you can do:

- Bring in pupils in an orderly fashion.

- Make them take outdoor coats off.

- Take the register out loud – don't be tempted to do it quietly without reading their names out.

- Have them respond 'Yes, Mrs/Mr . . .'.

- Check their uniform and that they are smart and clean (have they muddy shoes, clothes dishevelled etc.).

- Check for jewellery if that is the school rule.

- Clear off unauthorized absences.

- Set the tutor group a task to complete (this could be something like having five new spellings on board each day).

- Speak to individuals about causes for concern whilst others are engaged in the task.

- Have a 'Thought for the Day' that you put up on the board.

- Dismiss them in an orderly fashion and tell them to have a good morning or afternoon.

Dos and Don'ts of Behaviour Management

+ Be prepared to give up some of your time if they
  need you.

+ Do not see yourself as the enforcer on other
  teachers' behalf, but be the counsellor and supporter: this does not mean that you do not enforce
  your rules and expectations upon them when they
  are in your control.

+ Still be firm, but remember to be fair as well.

Bullying

I have deliberately included this, because it needs to
be in your mind every second of the day in any school.
As a form tutor, you may well be the person in whom a
pupil confides that s/he is being bullied. Schools are
breeding grounds for bullies and bullying. Do not be
under any illusions about that. Weren't you bullied at
school? I was and I can still remember the name of the
obnoxious youth who was responsible for the bullying
to this day. Very sadly, there have been some rightly
much-publicized incidents of youngsters taking their
own lives because of persistent bullying. Every teacher
has her/his part to play in ensuring as safe an environment as possible for every pupil.

First, if a pupil comes to you claiming that s/he is
being bullied, take it seriously, write it down, pass it on
to the Head of Year and assure the pupil that something
will be done about it. Then make sure that something is

done! If you have promised to do it, do it! If you have passed it on to a Head of Year, keep asking her/him what s/he has done about it. Make sure it is carried out. A record of the bullying incident, including names, dates and times must be kept on central file.

And finally, if it is a serious incident of bullying, the parent/carer must be informed and kept updated about what has happened and about any other developments. Then you, or the Head of Year, must regularly check with the bullied pupil to ensure that there has not been a re-occurrence. Do not believe that because that pupil has not been back to see you, everything is fine; it is often far worse, and now the pupil is really scared to tell you.

You cannot afford to get any of this wrong, you really can't! There is far too much at stake and, if a pupil is ever let down by you in a situation like this, it will be virtually impossible for her/him to ever fully trust you again. You must be thorough, diligent and super supportive. In this way, not only will that pupil's trust in you grow, but other pupils will trust you and also respect you as well.

How to Question Pupils and How to Tell when they are Lying

Both as a form tutor and as a classroom teacher, you will have to deal with situations that are brought to your attention. Please do not be a teacher who is in an almighty rush to pass the buck. Especially in your early years, you should see everything that comes your way as a learning opportunity, as well as one through which to gain valuable and priceless experience.

I really cannot remember where I read this, but it was in a book where there was a chapter on what to do when interrogating captured prisoners! I can almost read your mind at this moment, but bear with me. Lying is not as easy as you may think. Your brain is actually making a deliberate decision to not tell the truth. This is something that reflects in your body language, your sweat glands and, most importantly from our point of view, your eyes.

When questioning a pupil, what you say and how you say it is very important. If you are dealing with an allegation of theft or bullying, for instance, it is often useful to have another member of staff present. If they are present, it is better if one of you takes the lead and the other only infrequently interjects. Put the pupil at their ease and let her/him sit down facing you. Look at the general demeanour. Does s/he look confident or nervous? Comfortable or uneasy?

Do not tell her/him why s/he is there. Not at first. Ask the pupil why s/he believes s/he is there. If s/he suggests the real reason (the theft or the bullying), you are already a long way down the line in your investigation. More often than not, pupils play dumb. You need to make subtle hints and build these hints up until the pupil eventually accepts the reason for being there. If you are the questioner, sit directly in front of her/him and stare her/him in the eyes. Never break eye contact other than to watch her/his hands and general body language. *If s/he is lying, her/his eyes will flick to the left on answering your question.* S/he may also fidget, drop eye contact completely and just generally look very uneasy. If eyes flick to the right, it usually means they are recollecting a memory.

Be careful when questioning that you never accuse her/him. State repeatedly: 'I am not accusing you. However, your name has been brought to my attention . . .' Make sure you do this, because if you discover that s/he is innocent, you will not then have laid yourself open to an irate parent coming in after you. This is a very common error when dealing with a whole raft of incidents: teachers commit themselves too early and accuse the pupil personally. It is much better to stay detached and remain very objective. Take 'you' out of it and make her/him know that you are going on information received from another source or sources.

What I am about to tell you is very important, especially if you have taken the time, as you always should, to obtain as much corroborating evidence as possible. Remember, if you have no concrete evidence, it is imperative that you do remain objective and do not try to 'fit' the pupil up. However, there will be those occasions where you have the right person, and both you and the pupil know that, but s/he is simply not going to confess. What I have often done in these situations is to ensure that I have spoken to as many

165

Dos and Don'ts of Behaviour Management

other potential witnesses, and for each pupil to whom I have spoken, I write up what they have told me on a separate piece of paper, so that I end up having these individual pieces of paper in front of me. It doesn't matter about the exact detail of what is written on them, as long as it is obvious that they contain handwriting, and you tell the pupil whom you are questioning that these are verbal statements given to you by other pupils. You keep referring to these pieces of paper as evidence. You say: 'I have a number of witness statements.' You rifle through the sheets, giving them due consideration and deliberation.

It is also important at this point to repeat what I have already mentioned: you are not the accuser; these other pupils are the ones who have brought this to your attention! Never, under any circumstances mention the names of the pupils who have supplied the information and make sure that their names do not appear on the sheets. Then you can begin to key in specifics that you know occurred. This could be that the pupil was seen at the appropriate time and/or place, was alone there, had bragged about doing whatever it was that had occurred (this is very common amongst youngsters – they nearly always have to brag to someone else about what they have done!). Layer each one on top of the other. Keep looking at individual sheets and pretend to be carefully digesting what is written there. You are slowly building up more 'evidence' and pressure. Watch the reactions to your questioning and point-making.

The Management of Other Situations

This is potent and effective management of pupils. Believe me when I tell you that any pupil questioned by you in this manner will seriously think twice about taking you on in almost any situation. S/he will be both impressed by and in awe of your calm and your cool and considered approach. Take your time, deliver each question very carefully and deliberately and look her/him straight in the eye. Whether or not you manage to wring a confession out of her/him is almost secondary to the overall impression that you will have achieved.

And one last thing: I mentioned earlier the need to tell her/him that lying is the worst thing that s/he can do. And that is correct. You relate this to her/him in an educational manner. Even in really serious incidents, it is important to try and give the pupil an exit. Turn the situation round.

'Listen, Robert. What you have been accused of is serious. However, I am a teacher and I am in the business of education. People make mistakes. Sometimes we make the wrong decisions and the wrong choices. We have to own up to them, learn from them, accept the consequences, move on and make sure we don't do them again. You can't do any of those things if you lie to me. If you lie to me the consequences are going to be even more serious. What is worse, Robert, is that our relationship, which I value, will have been damaged.'

167

Dos and Don'ts of Behaviour Management

I use an approximation of this particular speech repeatedly. It pricks the youngster's conscience, it plays on her/his relationship with you, it gives some hope that all hell isn't about to descend upon her/him and it gives a chance to move on from the situation. And of course, it re-affirms your stance about the value you place on your relationship with her/him. All very potent! Be careful, however, that you do not do deals with the pupil; this is not your prerogative, especially if you are not a senior teacher. If s/he does confess to you, write everything down making sure that you record the fact that s/he has told the truth if that is the case and, if the offence warrants it, pass it on to a higher authority. So, if it had been the theft of a pen from your desk and you manage to obtain a frank confession from the pupil, you could deal with that yourself, write it up as you go along and pass the incident to a Head of Year marked 'For information only'. It may well be, like my school, that you have specific sheets that you fill out for a whole range of incidents and it will be one of these that you will complete.

If the pupil does tell the truth, even if it is eventually rather than straight away, thank the pupil and tell her/him that telling the truth has stood her/him in good stead. It is important to realize in all these situations that we are trying to educate, to move forward, to create a situation where the pupil will not do this again, to try and ensure that the pupil will make better decisions in the future. This will not be achieved if the teacher is heavy-handed, accusatory, confrontational, threatening or demeaning. The pupil has to feel that s/he can trust the person in front of her/him and that s/he wants to tell the truth, and that it is both the right thing to do and will help her/him.

8   What to Do If . . .

This is my final chapter. It is here to complete the picture. The pupils in your school, as well as the staff, both teaching and non-teaching, will often be influenced by how you deal with these unfortunate situations, as much as how you deal with the more routine ones. Always remember: take charge, be in control, stay calm, be confident and take a deep breath.

How to Deal with a Fight

I hope you never have to but, if you do, this will come in very useful. Fights can occur anywhere and at any time: in the classroom, or the corridor, in the yard. Pupils are attracted to fights like moths to a flame. If the fight is in a yard, you can bet your pension on the fact that it will draw a large crowd of baying onlookers and you might be the only member of staff around to deal with it. The common cry from pupils will normally be: 'Fight! Fight!'

So what do you do? First thing, and nothing to do with fighting or fights, buy a good whistle and carry it with you at all times. Do not leave it behind! If there is a fight in the yard and there are a few hundred pupils gathered around, you need to do several things and in this order:

- If you are alone, send a responsible pupil to get help in the shape of other colleagues.

- Never run to a fight; it only excites pupils more and you will not be as cool and calm as you need to be when you get there.

- As you approach where the fight is taking place, blow your whistle as loudly as you humanly can; the pupils watching will react to it and give you a chance to act.

- Unless you are physically bigger and superior and the protagonists have a healthy regard for you as a disciplinary figure, do not wade into the middle of the fight; you are likely to get injured yourself.

- Walk up to the fighters and in a firm voice say: 'I need you to stop now!' If you know their names, use them.

- If one fighter is losing and backing away, turn your attention to the aggressor; speak firmly and use 'I need' and the pupil's name if you know it.

171

Dos and Don'ts of Behaviour Management

- In this situation, you can physically put yourself between the two of them; hold your arms out straight, away from your body, towards the pupil who is the aggressor and keep talking calmly and firmly.

- Do not make physical contact; it will only make matters worse.

- If they try to get round you, while keeping your arms outstretched towards them, but not touching them, manoeuvre around so that you are still in between the two parties.

- With a bit of luck, other staff should be on the scene by now to help; if not keep this going, talking firmly and calmly all the time.

If the fight occurs in a classroom or corridor, the basic procedure as outlined above is still correct. Speak firmly, but calmly. Use their names if you know them. If you do not, there will be pupils there who will be able to tell you. Do not try and break them apart; wait until a natural distance occurs between them before stepping in between. Screaming or shouting will only excite them more. You need to be heard, but you must stay calm.

Verbal Abuse to Staff

I have worked in schools where they had a standard policy that any pupil swearing at a member of staff will be excluded for either the remainder of that day, if we can contact a parent/carer and the incident occurred during the morning session, or for the following day if the incident occurred in the afternoon, or we could not contact a parent/carer. Either way, it sends a very potent message to pupils that this kind of activity is simply not going to be tolerated. The pupil is always seen by either a Head of Year or me the following day.

Your school may not have such a policy; many schools do not because of the imposed need to reduce fixed-term exclusions. I personally believe that to be an error of judgment on their part. Nevertheless, whether there is such a policy or not, it does not take you, the teacher who has been abused, out of the equation. Whether the pupil has received an exclusion or not, repair work still needs to be done and the reason behind why the pupil has sworn at you has to be teased out.

I find that swearing at teachers occurs when some of the following conditions apply:

- ◆ The pupil is in an emotional state and you happen to be in the wrong place at the wrong time, probably saying the wrong thing as well!

- ◆ The pupil has been boxed in and not given an exit strategy.

- ◆ The pupil feels wronged by what has happened and is frustrated.

Dos and Don'ts of Behaviour Management

- Following on from that point, the pupil is emotionally illiterate and the only way s/he can voice her/his disapproval is by swearing.

- The teacher has not read the tell-tale signs and pushes a pupil too hard, when s/he should have eased off.

- And finally, the pupil is just being downright unpleasant for no other reason than s/he can be!

So what should you do? First, you are a teacher. Think educationally. Register strong disapproval of the language used and say: 'I think you owe me an apology.'

If the pupil gives you an apology, I would be tempted to have a few quiet words, register disappointment and then, depending on the circumstances, maybe let that be it. It is always better if you can resolve the matter satisfactorily yourself. Do not feel the necessity to report every incident that occurs between you and the pupils. The pupils will not respect you for it and it will ultimately undermine your authority.

If, however, the abuse is really bad and has to be reported, report it to a Head of Year or a senior member of staff. It is vital that you should make every effort to be there when the pupil is seen by this member of staff, and it is equally vital that the pupil should apologize to you. It is much more satisfactory if the pupil does not have to be made to apologize. An apology given freely is far better all round and pupils need to have this constantly inculcated in them. And, oh yes! If a pupil wants to apologize, please, please, do not refuse to accept it. You will be amazed at how many teachers do and it only drags out the resentment and the feud between them and that pupil. Please ask yourself who the adult is in this situation!

If a pupil swears at another pupil in your presence, you must make a decision about whether or not you were meant to hear, or even if the pupil swearing knew you were actually there. If you feel that the pupil was unaware of you, you need to check their use of bad language and probably leave the matter there with: 'I am disappointed in you. That was a disgusting outburst!'

However, if you feel that they knew you were there, then this is a challenge to your authority. You can say the same again to the pupil to register your disappointment, but you must also report the incident to a Head of Year and tell the pupil that you are going to do so.

Physical Assault on a Member of Staff

I sincerely hope that this never, ever occurs to you and I must stress now that these are infrequent events. The best advice is to know your pupils, know their potential for disruption or outbursts and read the signs. Most 'assaults' involve a push or shove to a teacher. Again, this will be born out of frustration and anger and an inability on the pupil's part to resolve the matter in an intellectual fashion. In short, it is an amygdala response. Remember them?

If you are pushed or assaulted in any other way by a pupil, it really must be reported and a higher authority is going to have to determine what the punishment will be, not you. It could end up with the pupil being permanently excluded and this may well be upsetting for you, but you have to keep a sense of proportion here: what signal does it send to the rest of the pupil population if this action is not taken, and what message does it send to members of staff as well? That abiding character Spock from *Star Trek* said in 'The Wrath of Khan' something to the effect: 'The needs of the many outweigh the needs of the few and always outweigh the needs of the one.' And when staff like me have to make these judgments about whether a permanent exclusion is the correct decision – and they are rarely easy to make – this is generally the underpinning rationale.

9   A Final Word

At the end of the day, you are your own person and you will develop your own strategies. However, the ones I have outlined to you do work, they work extremely effectively. If you are a teacher already and you are experiencing problems, I strongly recommend that you adopt these and put them into practice. If you are about to become a teacher, it would be very wise to follow them to the letter – all of them.

As you become more experienced, so you will be able to adapt and modify. You will soon see which ones really work for you and develop your own inimitable way of employing them. This is important because we do not want to produce teacher-clones. You are an individual with your own personality and mannerisms. Never lose sight of that: indeed, treasure it!

If I had to summarize and state which of the points I have made are absolute necessities, then this would be the shortlist:

Dos and Don'ts of Behaviour Management

- Be confident.

- Be prepared.

- Be respectful.

- Be quiet.

- Be caring.

- Be firm and fair.

- Be someone pupils respect and trust.

However, remember you are not their friend. That is not to say that some of them will not see you as such, but you are not. You are a trusted adult; you are a counsellor; you are an adviser; you are a confidant; you are friendly; you are caring. But you must keep your distance! Familiarity breeds contempt and you must guard against it. Pupils do not necessarily have the maturity or the experience to handle a relationship with a teacher which gets too familiar.

So with those thoughts in your head, you only need to remember one more thing and the most important of all: **HAVE A GOOD SENSE OF HUMOUR!**

I wish you all the very best. There is no joy in trying to teach constantly disruptive classes. However, there is immense pleasure in seeing youngsters learn in your classroom as a result of your teaching. I hope that I have given you some essential guidelines on how to make sure that poor behaviour does not happen or will cease to be the case in future. And, if it does, you will have the wherewithal to combat it. I also hope that I have given you sound overall advice on the various elements and complexities that contribute to making this the uplifting profession it truly can, and should, be.

Good Luck!